Jaw-Dropping Fun Facts About Universal Family Secrets, Scandals, Deceptions, and Deathbed Confessions

"Dying to Get This Off My Chest - Hilariously Shocking

Final Confessions and Deathbed Secrets"

Rebecca von Pits
&
Matt Robin

Jaw-Dropping Fun Facts About Universal Family Secrets, Scandals, Deceptions, and Deathbed Confessions

"Dying to Get This Off My Chest - Hilariously Shocking Final Confessions and Deathbed Secrets"

CROSSBORDER
PUBLISHERS LLC

New York, London, Quebec

Contents

Introduction

At long last, the world's most scandalously amusing skeletons are coming out of the closet – and trust me, they're tap-dancing on their way out. In these pages, we're about to uncork a vintage bottle of family secrets so effervescently outrageous that even your stiffest upper lip won't know whether to tremble in shock or curl into a smirk. Consider this a mock-serious exposé on the grand tradition of whispering "I have *something* to confess..." just as the will is being read. And like any good British tea, we're serving it with a twist of sarcasm, a pinch of wit, and maybe a *tiny* paper umbrella for good measure.

Now, you might be thinking (in a delightfully aghast tone), *"Surely my family has never harbored deceptions worthy of a telenovela!"* Oh, sweet summer child, think again. *Jaw-Dropping Fun Facts About Universal Family Secrets* is exactly what it claims: a riotous compendium of truth bombs from families big and small, celebrity-level and suburban-ordinary. We're spilling the Earl Grey on everything from decades-old double lives to last-minute deathbed truth-bombs that would make even Sherlock Holmes do a double take. The tone here may be cheeky and satirical, but the revelations? Absolutely real (and really absurd).

For instance, brace yourself to encounter stories such as:

- **The Sweet Grandmother with a Secret Past:** That adorable Nana knitting you sweaters? She might casually confess to a former life as a **black-market marmalade dealer** – *and* insist it was for Queen and country.

- **The Suburban Saint Turned Sinner:** Picture the PTA president down the street. Now imagine discovering she once faked an alien abduction **just** to cover up a Vegas marriage. (Yes, Margaret, we're onto you.)

- **The Celebrity Cousin's Final Curtain Call:** Then there's the almost-famous actor uncle whose dying wish was to reveal he'd been **lip-syncing his Shakespeare** his entire career – oh, the drama!

For the record, those shockers are merely the warm-up acts in this carnival of candor and chaos. Sound crazy? Indeed. True? Let's just say names have been changed to protect the *guilty*.

Each chapter is a front-row seat to familial theater at its finest (and its most hilariously dysfunctional). And as your self-appointed tour guide through this cavalcade of cozy little nightmares, we promise to navigate with a flair for the dramatic and a wink of solidarity. After all, who among us hasn't suspected our perfectly normal family might be one poorly-timed confession away from a soap opera Christmas special?

So, welcome to the inner circle. Pull up a chair (preferably a throne draped in plastic cover – things *will* get messy) and prepare to bond with humanity's universal guilty pleasure: other people's secrets. You'll laugh, you'll gasp, and you might never look at your own family the same way again.

But hey, keep calm and carry on reading – every family has its quirks, darling. Ours just happen to be printed in full, glossy color for your reading pleasure. Now take a deep breath, stiffen your resolve (and maybe your drink), and turn the page – the secrets await.

Rebecca and myself Matt (Your Cheeky Confidants) are glad you are here, and thank you in advance for reading.

Chapter 1

Killer Confessions – Final Acts of Murderous Guilt

In the world of true crime, justice sometimes takes its sweet time – decades, even – only to arrive in the most dramatic fashion possible: via a last-gasp confession. You might think murderers would take their secrets to the grave, but as these five tales show, sometimes they just can't resist a final act twist. It's as if guilt weighs on the soul like an overpacked carry-on, and at the end, these folks just had to unload – consequences be darned. From a repentant Klansman's dying regret to a not-so-dead convict blurting out "Oops, I did it," each story here is a jaw-dropping, head-shaking lesson in late-stage truth-telling. And yes, we'll be dishing it out with a side of wit and satire – because if we don't laugh, we'd probably cry (or shudder). So grab your popcorn and your moral compass, and let's dive into these killer confessions that prove fact can be stranger (and wilder) than fiction.

1.1 The Klansman's Last Regret – Henry Alexander's Final Change of Heart

When you picture a Ku Klux Klansman experiencing a change of heart, you might imagine a Hallmark movie with a highly unlikely plot. But Henry Alexander's real-life deathbed confession is about as close as we get: a villain's Darth Vader moment of redemption, minus the John

Williams soundtrack. Alexander was a longtime Klansman, the kind of guy who spent the 1950s doing unspeakably awful things in the name of white supremacy. One of those heinous deeds was the 1957 murder of Willie Edwards Jr., a 24-year-old Black husband and father. Edwards was forced at gunpoint to jump off a bridge in Montgomery, Alabama – a crime that went unpunished for decades. Alexander had always denied involvement (because of course he did – hate crimes aren't exactly the kind of hobby you brag about at family dinners). But as he lay dying of lung cancer in 1993, Alexander suddenly felt the urge to unburden his conscience. In a twist no one saw coming – especially not his wife, Diane – he blurted out that *yes*, he had been the ringleader all along.

This wasn't some soft, sanitized apology either. According to his widow, the dying Alexander admitted he concocted the entire scenario that led to Willie Edwards' death. Why? *"I just wanted to be important,"* he confessed, lamenting that he'd lied about Edwards "making a pass at a white woman" to impress his fellow Klansmen. In other words, he basically started a lethal rumor because he was insecure about his KKK street cred. With death staring him in the face, Alexander finally expressed real remorse, telling his wife, *"That man never hurt anybody. I was just running my mouth. I caused it."* It's the kind of line you'd expect from a sad old character in a Southern Gothic novel, not from a lifelong bigot whose résumé included church bombings.

Diane Alexander, who never even knew her common-law husband was involved in the Edwards case, had to be *gobsmacked*. One can only imagine her expression: *"Honey, you choose now to tell me you did a murder?!"*

The unexpected confession came roughly three weeks before Henry Alexander died, giving just enough time for the truth to finally breathe after 36 years in the dark. (Two decades earlier, prosecutors had actually charged Alexander and three other men, but a judge tossed the case because they couldn't prove exactly how Edwards died – the irony being that the victim's terror-induced plunge left a legal loophole.) Alexander's last-minute honesty didn't lead to a trial – he was beyond earthly justice at that point – but it delivered something almost as powerful: closure. Willie Edwards Jr.'s family, who had endured decades of not knowing, finally learned what happened and heard an admission of guilt (albeit secondhand). In a way, it was a sliver of justice delivered from beyond the legal grave.

From a broader perspective, Henry Alexander's deathbed admission is a stark reminder that even people steeped in hate can feel the weight of their sins at the bitter end. It's like the ultimate anticlimax for a villain – no shootout, no blazing inferno, just an old man in a hospital bed whispering *"I did wrong."* If this were a movie, the audience would be left with an uneasy catharsis: satisfaction that the truth came out, tempered by disgust that it took so long. The moral? Prejudice and violence may silence their victims, but they can also haunt the perpetrators to their last breath. Alexander spent decades living a lie, only to have the truth claw its way out at the eleventh hour. In his final chapter, the big bad Klansman didn't seek glory or martyrdom – he sought forgiveness, or at least a release from guilt. Unexpected? Absolutely. But as we're about to see, he's far from the only dying criminal who decided honesty was the best (and last) policy.

1.2 Cold Case Closed from the Grave – Larry Webb Solves His Own Crime

Not all deathbed confessions are about repentance – some are practically **true-crime lifehacks**. Case in point: Larry Webb, an 80-year-old West Virginia man who in April 2024 decided to do something the FBI and countless detectives hadn't been able to do for 24 years – solve the mystery of what happened to Susan Carter and her 10-year-old daughter Natasha "Alex" Carter. This cold case was colder than an Appalachian winter. Susan and Alex vanished way back in August 2000 without a trace. For years, their disappearance was the stuff of local lore and *Unsolved Mysteries* reruns. Tips went nowhere and leads grew stale. Little did anyone suspect that the culprit was right under their noses the whole time, living out his golden years in the very same community.

Larry Webb had actually been on law enforcement's radar – during a 2022 search of his property, investigators found a bullet embedded in the wall of a bedroom where 10-year-old Alex had stayed, and it even had her DNA on it. That discovery led to Webb's indictment in late 2023 and ramped up the pressure on the ailing octogenarian. With his health failing and a trial looming, it seems Webb decided to take an *unorthodox shortcut*: on his deathbed, he simply spilled the beans. Investigators visited him in a nursing home in April 2024, and as he lay dying, Webb confessed to shooting Susan and Alex back in 2000 and burying their bodies in his backyard. It was as if the Grim Reaper held out a microphone and Webb went, *"Okay, fine, I did it – here's where they are."* For the Carter family and the community, that confession was nothing short of miraculous. Within hours of his final breaths, authorities were digging up Webb's property –

and sure enough, they uncovered human remains believed to be the long-lost mother and daughter. After 24 years of agony, the case cracked open *literally* overnight.

Picture the scene: one moment the man's on a gurney gasping, "I killed them, they're in the yard," and by that evening the crime scene techs are swarming his backyard like it's an archaeological dig with a very fresh tip-off. It's almost cinematic – if this were a movie, you'd call it too convenient. But truth sometimes outdoes fiction. Thanks to Webb's last-minute bout of conscience (or fear of divine judgment – take your pick), a grieving father finally got the closure he'd been longing for. Rick Lafferty, Alex Carter's father, said he felt a mix of sadness, happiness and relief at *finally* knowing what happened and being able to "bring my baby home" for a proper goodbye. Those words are heavy; they reflect a parent's nightmare ending with at least the solace of certainty.

Now, let's not paint Larry Webb as any kind of hero here – he was the murderer, after all. In fact, his motives were as banal as they come. Reports revealed that Susan, who was staying with Webb during a custody battle with her ex, had a blow-up with him when he noticed some of his money had gone missing. In a fit of anger, Webb shot the 41-year-old mother, then realized he had a witness – little Alex – and chillingly decided to eliminate her too. He described wrapping their bodies in bed linens, keeping them in his house for two days while he dug a shallow grave, and then burying them like some macabre DIY project. That's straight-up evil. The fact that he let everyone suffer in uncertainty for over two decades, only to confess at the eleventh hour, suggests that guilt (or the prospect of meeting his maker) finally gnawed through his defenses.

Either way, Webb's confession closed a chapter that had tormented a community since the turn of the millennium. It's a rare instance where a deathbed confession directly led to tangible justice – bodies found, case solved. Most cold cases would kill for a breakthrough like that (pardon the expression). In true 21st-century fashion, the whole thing was confirmed in a media news conference, with officials essentially saying, "Yep, he did it, and here's the proof." If this were an episode of *CSI*, you might roll your eyes; in real life, you stand back and marvel at the bizarre, bittersweet truth. The lesson here? Some secrets really *can't* be kept forever – even if you've gotten away with murder for 24 years. In the end, Larry Webb died a confessed killer, but at least he didn't die a lying one. He solved his own crime just in time to face a higher court, as it were, leaving the rest of us to marvel at a cold case closed from beyond the grave.

1.3 Old Hollywood Whodunit Solved – Margaret Gibson's Silent Era Secret

The iconic Hollywood Sign has seen plenty of scandals in its time – even a murder mystery that took 42 years to get its "big reveal." In the annals of Hollywood scandals, the 1922 murder of film director William Desmond Taylor is legendary. It had everything: a famous victim, starlet suspects, love triangles, and decades of wild speculation. It was the original Tinseltown whodunit – a real-life noir that outlasted the silent films themselves. By the 1960s, Taylor's murder was a cold case as chilly as a *martini at Musso*

& Frank, one of those mysteries old studio guards might gossip about when they thought no one was listening. Then, in 1964, a plot twist straight out of a pulp novel dropped into their laps: a forgotten silent-film actress named Margaret Gibson confessed on her deathbed that she was the one who killed Taylor all along. Imagine the collective gasp. It was as if a bit player suddenly stole the final scene, gasping *"It was me!"* before the credits rolled.

Margaret Gibson, who by that time was living under an alias and far removed from Hollywood, had never even been a suspect in the original investigation. Back in the day, the police and press had fixated on more glamorous figures: Taylor's close friend (and rumored sweetheart) Mabel Normand, young ingénue Mary Miles Minter with her obsessive crush, and even Minter's domineering mother, Charlotte Shelby (a mom-ager so formidable she made Mama Rose look like Mother Teresa). Gibson's name was buried deep in the cast list of Taylor's life – practically an *extra*. Sure, she had acted with Taylor briefly in 1914, but investigators saw no connection after that. So her late-in-life confession came out of nowhere – like a former backup singer at a reunion show suddenly announcing she wrote all the band's hits. According to accounts of that fateful day, as Gibson lay dying of a heart attack at age 70, she became deeply agitated and summoned a priest to hear her final confession. In those last moments, she reportedly spilled the secret she'd kept for 42 years: *"I killed William Desmond Taylor."* (Cue the dramatic close-up and stunned silence.)

Now, Hollywood being Hollywood, this revelation raised as many questions as it answered. Gibson didn't give a detailed narrative – no juicy monologue explaining the *how* and *why* of the deed. And because she waited until 1964, all the original police files and physical evidence had long since vanished (the LAPD's records on the Taylor case mysteriously disappeared by 1940). Talk about frustrating: someone finally yells "Cut, we have the killer!" but half the crew has gone home. However, those who've studied the case note that nothing in Gibson's confession blatantly contradicted the known facts of the crime. In fact, it oddly *fit*. Perhaps Gibson had a motive that flew under the radar – some secret affair or simmering grudge? Perhaps she was at Taylor's bungalow that evening and an argument spiraled out of control. With no way to verify her story, the world was left to take her at her word, as if *she* were the final authority on a mystery that had stumped everyone else.

So did this deathbed bombshell solve the Taylor murder? In a court-of-law sense, no – the confession came too late to be proved or prosecuted. The Los Angeles Police weren't about to reopen a 42-year-old case on the say-so of a dying woman, especially one who had flown completely under their radar. But in the court of public opinion and Hollywood lore, Gibson's confession is often cited as the likely resolution of Taylor's murder. At long last, a plausible answer emerged for one of early Hollywood's greatest unsolved crimes. For the old-timers who remembered the case, it was vindication (and maybe a bit of a *buzzkill* for the conspiracy theorists who'd spun other elaborate scenarios). The Taylor murder, it seems, had been an insider job by a fellow denizen of silent-era Hollywood – not a jealous mogul or mob hitman or crazed fan, but an actress who had slipped through the cracks of history.

To put it in modern terms, it's as if a minor character actor from a Marvel movie suddenly tweeted a confession to an unsolved 1980s Hollywood murder – the world would freak out, right? In 1964, there was no TMZ or Twitter, but the few people privy to Gibson's confession must have been floored. (One can imagine the priest needing a stiff drink afterwards, muttering, *"You won't believe what I just heard..."*) The Gibson confession offers a few takeaways: first, Hollywood secrets have a way of coming out, even if it's decades later in a whisper to a priest. Second, guilt doesn't care about fame – from ex-Klansmen to faded starlets with killer secrets, a guilty conscience can drive anyone to speak up at the very end. The rich and famous aren't so different from the rest of us when it comes to remorse; they just have better storylines. In this case, a long-forgotten actress got one final close-up – not on the silver screen, but on her deathbed – and delivered the closing line to a saga that had outlived the silent films. It's dark, it's dramatic, and it's quintessential Hollywood.

1.4 Biker's Deadly Secret in the Swamp – The Amy Billig Mystery

Every parent's worst nightmare is a child who vanishes without a trace. For Susan Billig, that nightmare began on March 5, 1974, when her 17-year-old daughter Amy left home in Coconut Grove, Florida and never came back. For 24 agonizing years, Susan chased every lead, every rumor – no matter how bizarre or disturbing – hoping to find Amy alive. It had all the makings of a gritty 1970s crime drama – a rebellious teen and the specter of biker gangs – but no happy ending was in sight. Through it all, Susan Billig refused to give up hope, living in that torturous limbo between hope and grief. Fast forward to the late 1990s, and the case was ice-cold – until a dying man's conscience finally thawed it out.

The vast Florida Everglades have swallowed many secrets – and for decades, the fate of Amy Billig was one of them. The breakthrough came in 1998 courtesy of Paul Branch, a former "enforcer" for the Pagans motorcycle gang and a man who, it turns out, had known the truth about Amy's fate all along. As Branch lay dying of cancer at his home in Virginia, he decided to come clean in true Sons of Anarchy style. He confessed to his wife (who relayed it to investigators) that back in 1974 the Pagans had abducted Amy Billig off the street and taken her to a "party" out in the Florida Everglades. Now, if you hear "party in the Everglades" and imagine bonfires and beer, think again – this was more like a scene from a horror film. Branch's deathbed confession painted a gut-wrenching picture: Amy was *drugged*, gang-raped by a horde of bikers, and ultimately killed, her slight 17-year-old body dumped in the swamp like garbage once the criminals were done. All of it happened within hours of her abduction. It's hard to overstate how horrific that is. Detective Jack Calvar, the lead investigator on the case, later said Branch's confession included dozens of details that matched what police had suspected over the years. But hearing it laid out in full must have been a punch to the gut nonetheless.

For Susan Billig, Branch's confession was both devastating and strangely vindicating. For years she had chased rumors that Amy had been taken by a biker gang, even putting herself in danger following those leads across the country. She held onto the belief that her daughter might be alive somewhere, perhaps brainwashed or trapped in a hidden life. Branch's final revelation extinguished that last flicker of hope – but it also ended the uncertainty. As painful as it was to learn the gruesome truth, there was grim solace in *knowing*. In early 1998, Susan Billig, then in her early 70s, finally accepted that her daughter was never coming home. She invited friends to a memorial service for Amy – essentially a funeral, 24 years delayed. Wearing black, Susan managed to smile as each guest arrived at her Coconut Grove home. *"Having my friends around me is a tremendous sense of peace,"* she said. *"We have to laugh and be merry because Amy would have wanted us to."* If you're looking for grace amid tragedy, there it is – a mother choosing to celebrate her child's life rather than only mourn the horrible way it ended.

Paul Branch didn't exactly deliver justice with his deathbed admission – he named no names besides his own, and he passed away right after unburdening himself, beyond the reach of any law. Police believe the bikers disposed of Amy's body in the alligator-infested wetlands, meaning her remains will likely never be found. It's a heartbreaking coda: after all of Susan's searching, there would be no physical closure, no grave to visit – only a story of unspeakable cruelty and a belated confession. Still, the mystery that haunted South Florida for a generation was essentially solved, not by forensic science or a lucky tip, but by a guilty conscience and the oldest truth serum of all: imminent mortality. Branch's wife did the right thing by immediately reporting his confession to authorities, and Detective Calvar was able to corroborate much of the tale through other interviews and evidence. Tragically, there was nothing more to be done

— the sad answer remained the same: Amy was gone, and the swamp had swallowed the secret.

If there's any lesson in this horrific tale, it's a testament to a parent's love and the strange ways fate can finally cough up answers. Susan Billig's unwavering resolve is almost heroic — she spent nearly a quarter-century chasing phantoms and never gave up. In the end, she got the truth, delivered in the most brutal manner imaginable. It's not the kind of closure anyone would wish for, but it was the only kind left to have. And for the rest of us, there's a takeaway too: if someone is dying and suddenly wants to confess something, listen up — you never know if you'll hear the key to a mystery. The Amy Billig case will forever remain a cautionary tale — sometimes all the money, fame, or effort in the world can't bring closure until fate (or a biker's guilty conscience) intervenes. It's a bitter pill wrapped in a small mercy: at least now the Billig family *knows* what became of Amy, and her soul — wherever it is — can finally be at peace.

1.5 The "Oops, I Didn't Die" Confession – James Washington's Big Mouth

Most deathbed confessions are made by people who, you know, actually die. But James Washington isn't most people. This Nashville inmate managed to pull off one of the darkly funniest faux pas in criminal history: he confessed to murder during what he *thought* was his final hour, survived, and then had to live with the fallout. It's like a twisted version of Monty Python's "I'm not dead yet!" sketch — except instead of a plague victim on a cart, we've got a convicted felon on a hospital gurney blurting out guilt. The year was 2009, and Washington, then 46, was serving time in a Tennessee prison for an unrelated crime. One day he suffered a massive heart attack or seizure (accounts vary) and truly believed he was at death's door. In that panicky moment, Washington beckoned a prison guard, James Tomlinson, closer. *"I have something to tell you,"* he gasped. *"I have to get this off my conscience... I killed somebody."* He then elaborated that he had murdered a woman named Joyce Goodener back in 1995, beating her to death. Now, this was a jaw-dropper: Goodener, 35, had indeed been brutally killed in 1995 – stabbed, bludgeoned with a cinder block, then rolled in a rug and set on fire in an abandoned house. It was an unsolved cold case, and Washington had long been a suspect (he knew the victim, and investigators always thought his alibi stank), but they never had enough evidence to charge him. Yet here he was, apparently on his deathbed, freely admitting *"I did it."* Case closed! Justice served! High-fives all around the homicide unit, right?

Not so fast. In a cosmic twist that's equal parts tragic and farcical, James Washington did *not* die. He survived the medical episode and lived to see another day – and that meant the authorities were very much interested in holding him to his sudden burst of honesty. Once Washington recovered and realized he was going to keep on living, he desperately tried to *uncorrect* the record. He told anyone who would listen that he'd been hallucinating when he confessed, that the medications and trauma had made him imagine things. Nice try, but that's not how it works. Hallucinations might make you see pink elephants; they usually don't make you invent highly specific unsolved murders that you just happen to have intimate knowledge of. The prison guard, Tomlinson, testified that Washington was plenty lucid when he made the statement

– lucid enough to look him in the eye and say, *"I beat her to death."* In fact, as soon as Washington spilled the beans, the guard immediately reported it to his supervisor, so there was a written record almost on the spot. Washington's attempt to retract his confession was about as convincing as claiming the dog ate his homework.

Washington's ill-timed truth-telling finally allowed Nashville authorities to close the book on Joyce Goodener's murder. In 2012, after a trial that must have been equal parts riveting and absurd, a jury convicted him of the 1995 murder and a judge handed down a life sentence. The key evidence? That deathbed confession (or should we call it a near-deathbed confession?). They had no DNA, no eyewitness – just his own big mouth, which turned out to be more effective than a CSI kit. Tomlinson, the guard, recounted in court how Washington had literally reached up from what he thought was his deathbed to confess. The defense, understandably scrambling, tried to argue that Washington had been out of his head from drugs and illness. But the jury didn't buy it. Investigators, who had suspected him all along, finally had the smoking gun – or rather, the smoking tongue. As one prosecutor put it, *"It was a detailed, undeniable, unconflicted confession... it aligned with the evidence we had."* (In other words: nice of you to solve our case for us, sir.)

Let's appreciate the irony here. James Washington nearly gamed the system – he aimed to ease his conscience on the way out of this world, avoiding any human punishment while scoring points with the divine (or so he thought). But he misjudged his expiration date. Imagine his face when he opened his eyes in the hospital, likely thinking, *"Oh crap, did I say that out loud?"* It was the ultimate you-can't-take-it-back moment. It's like sending a drunken text you can't unsend, except the text was "I'm a murderer" and the recipient was the State of Tennessee. Needless to say, the prosecutors were *thrilled*. This was a cold case that fell into their laps gift-wrapped. And Washington had no one to blame but himself.

In a roundabout way, you could say Washington's conscience did what the cops couldn't. Joyce Goodener's family finally saw her killer held accountable, even if justice arrived 17 years late. And Washington? He's now serving life in prison, presumably with plenty of time to reflect on the epic oopsie that put him there. If he ever feels the urge to confess something again, you can bet he'll check his own pulse first to be absolutely sure he's a goner. The "Oops, I Didn't Die" confession is a tale as old as… well, nothing quite like this has happened before, to be honest. But it teaches a simple lesson: if you're going to confess your darkest secret, be 100% sure you won't be around to regret it. Otherwise, your words *will* come back to haunt you – and by "haunt," I mean land you in prison for the rest of your natural life. As a final chapter in our gallery of killer confessions, you have to admit it's perversely satisfying: in this case, truth got the last laugh, and justice – however delayed – was finally served. And somewhere, perhaps, Joyce Goodener can rest a little easier, thanks to a bad guy who spoke up too soon and lived to regret it.

Chapter 2

Fortune and Folly – Inheritance Secrets and Last Laugh Wills

Picture a sun-soaked Beverly Hills terrace at brunch, mimosas sparkling and gossip flowing as freely as the champagne. Here, between bites of avocado toast and finger sandwiches, a storyteller (let's call them a slightly tipsy family friend) regales the table with outrageous tales of last wills and testaments. These aren't your run-of-the-mill estate plans – they're final acts of drama so absurd and juicy that even the Kardashians would raise impeccably groomed eyebrows. Lean in, top off that mimosa, and prepare for *Fortune and Folly*, a whirlwind of inheritance secrets and last laugh wills that prove truth is not only stranger than fiction, it's wittier and far more vindictive.

2.1 Ghosts of Grudges Past

Our brunch raconteur dabs their lips with a linen napkin and launches into the first story, a nineteenth-century zinger that sets the tone. Heinrich "Henry" Heine, a German poet known for his sharp wit, decided to script one last joke at his wife's expense – from beyond the grave. When Heine died in 1856, he left his entire estate to his wife, Mathilde, on one spiteful condition: she only gets the money *if* she remarries. Why on earth would a husband's dying wish be for his beloved to find a new husband? Heine quipped that this way "there will be at least one man to regret my death". Yes, you heard that right – the man orchestrated a *posthumous mic drop*, ensuring some poor sap would curse his name while paying the bills. It's the kind of dark marital humor that makes you choke on your croissant: equal parts *awful* and *ingenious*. If this were a reality show reveal, we'd cut to the widow's stunned face as the notary reads that clause – a scene juicier than any *Real Housewives* finale.

Heine's last laugh condition feels like something a petty ex would tweet if Twitter existed in the 1850s – a sort of Victorian subtweet in legalese. One can almost imagine Elon Musk taking notes for a future stunt ("Marry my ex and *then* you can have my Tesla stocks, haha, just kidding... unless?"). At our table, someone snorts into their latte, noting that Heine essentially left a romantic booby trap. The lesson? Even a famous poet couldn't resist a final act of snarky revenge. It's the *pettiness of revenge from beyond* made legendary, a reminder that some spouses will seize the last word *even after* "till death do us part." And if you think that's the peak of marital pettiness, hold onto your sunhat – we're just getting started.

With Heine's story warming up the room (and prompting at least one brunch guest to quip, "Better be nice to your hubby or he'll Henry Heine you"), our storyteller segues to another tale of matrimonial spite, this time with an extra dash of misogyny. Meet T.M. Zink, an Iowa lawyer who passed in 1930 with a will so bitter it could curdle the cream in your coffee. Zink's will didn't bother with witty one-liners; it was more of a manifesto. He disinherited his wife entirely and left his daughter a whopping five dollars – essentially enough for a sandwich, even back then. Five bucks to his own daughter! (At least he didn't require her to remarry for it.) The rest of Zink's estate, about $100,000 (think well over a million in today's dollars), was to be locked away in trust for 75 years to fund his life's grand vision: a "womanless library". Yes, you read that correctly. This man wanted to endow a library from which women were *permanently banned.* It was the ultimate He-Man Woman-Haters Club writ large, a literary man-cave funded from beyond the grave.

Our brunch group is aghast and amused. "Was this guy real?!" gasps a guest, half-laughing. Oh yes, Mr. Zink was dead serious. His will decreed that *"No woman shall at any time, under any pretense… be allowed inside the library"* he was funding. He forbade any female involvement – even the books had to be by male authors only. Over the door would loom a sign: "No Woman Admitted". It's as if he tried to weaponize his last will to make the entire world as bitter as his divorce. One bruncher jokes that Zink must be the patron saint of internet trolls and incels, born a century too early. His hatred was so intense he even explained it at length in his will (truly an *eccentric* final statement): *"My intense hatred of women is not of recent origin… but is the result of my experiences with women"* and so on. Imagine being that committed to misogyny – the man basically Ghost-wrote (pun intended) a dystopian library proposal that makes *The Handmaid's Tale* look subtle.

Of course, in a twist worthy of a satirical novel, Zink's grand scheme didn't pan out. His horrified family swiftly contested the will on grounds of insanity, and the courts agreed, declaring him of unsound mind. The "womanless library" never saw the light of day, and Zink's daughter ended up inheriting the estate instead. (In cosmic karma, that must have really made his ashes stir.) One can't help but picture the daughter Margretta walking into a *very* co-ed library funded by dear old Dad's money and checking out *Little Women* with a triumphant smile. The tale of T.M. Zink is a stark illustration of the lengths to which bitterness can drive a person – he tried to reach out from the afterlife to enforce his grudge, only to be laughed out of court and end up funding the very people he loathed. If Heinrich Heine's will was a cheeky taunt, Zink's was an outright battle cry in the war of the sexes. Both underscore the same family lesson: even six feet under, some folks just *can't let things go*. They had fortune, and by golly, they'd wield folly like a sword.

2.2 Riches Gone to the Dogs

By now the brunch table is divided between cackling at these ghostly grudges and wide-eyed disbelief. One guest fans themselves with the dessert menu, chiming in: "This is like an episode of *Succession* meets *The Twilight Zone*." Our storyteller grins. "Speaking of succession," they say, "let's talk about the *Queen of Mean*." Enter Leona Helmsley, the billionaire hotelier whose idea of *who* should inherit might make even Logan Roy (of *Succession* fame) say, "Whoa, that's cold." Helmsley earned her nickname by terrorizing hotel staff and proclaiming "only the little people pay taxes" – subtle, right? When she died in 2007, she put on one last show-stopping display of *the absurdity of human vanity*. Rather than spreading her $4 billion fortune among *all* her human heirs or a worthy cause, Leona decided to spend it caring for dogs. Yes, dogs – those tail-wagging, flea-scratching, furry children we all secretly prefer to humans sometimes. In Helmsley's case, she *really* preferred them. In an earlier draft, she had considered leaving her fortune to the poor, but apparently thought better of it and opted for canine-kind instead. (Perhaps philanthropy didn't match her outfit that season.)

Helmsley's most infamous bequest was to her own pet Maltese, a fluffy little thing ironically named Trouble. To this pampered pup she left a whopping $12 million trust fund. Meanwhile, two of her grandchildren got completely cut out of her will – *zero, zilch, nada* – and the other grandkids were reportedly only allowed to inherit if they paid a visit to their father's grave *once a year*. (Nothing says family love like annual mandated cemetery trips for cash, right?) It's as if Leona treated her will like a reality TV reunion special: rewarding the loyal, punishing the perceived traitors, and causing maximum drama. One brunch guest jokes, "At least she didn't make the grandkids fight to the death for the inheritance Hunger Games-style." True, Helmsley stopped short of a literal arena. But in the court of public opinion, she sparked an uproar. Her poor dog *Trouble* had to go into hiding, guarded like a celebrity, because – I am not kidding – he received death and kidnap threats from outraged humans who apparently drew the line at a canine multi-millionaire. Imagine hating a dog for inheriting money. (Then again, imagine being the dog, suddenly richer than Mariah Carey, wondering why the dog park paparazzi are hounding you.)

If this sounds like something out of a satirical film, the brunch crew quickly supplies casting: Perhaps Meryl Streep or Glenn Close as Helmsley (a touch of *Cruella de Vil*, minus the dalmatians – Helmsley preferred Maltese). We sip our drinks and marvel at the sheer vanity and odd logic. Helmsley essentially said, "I trust *no one* with my money except my dog (and maybe my brother, who got named caretaker of the dog's trust)." It's an extreme example of how wealth can insulate and isolate — she valued *loyalty*, and in her world, who's more loyal than man's best friend? Even Oprah Winfrey, known for her generosity, has reportedly set aside $30 million for her dogs' care (she's still alive and *very* loved, so no pitchforks there). But Helmsley's move was unprecedented in scale and pettiness. The tabloids had a field day dubbing the pooch "Richie Rich dog" and quipping that Trouble had a richer diet than most humans. Indeed, part of that $12 million was meant for the dog's upkeep — think luxury kibble and personal security. A judge later *slashed* Trouble's inheritance to $2 million (poor pup, how will he survive on that?), reasoning that perhaps $12M was a tad excessive for chew toys and dog biscuits. Helmsley's will stands as a gilded monument to vanity and misplaced affection, a kind of posthumous punchline: she literally sent her fortune to the dogs. If the *pettiness of revenge* was Heine's legacy, Helmsley's is the *theatre of the absurd* — an eccentric "because I can" gesture that left everyone barking.

Around our brunch table, someone does an impromptu impression of a lawyer reading Helmsley's will: *"To my dog, I leave twelve million dollars. To my grandchildren, I leave the possibility of money if they prove once a year they can locate a tombstone in Westchester. Good luck, kids."* The laughter is as fizzy as the champagne. It's the kind of story that makes you double-check grandma's will for any surprise pet trusts. The family lesson here practically writes itself: don't anger Grandma, or Fluffy might end up with your college fund. And perhaps a deeper lesson about vanity and love – Helmsley's fortune couldn't buy genuine affection, so she engineered loyalty in her will, a final power play by a woman who had to have the last word (or bark).

2.3 Stranger Than Fiction Inheritance

Just when the mimosas are running low and we think we've heard it all, our storyteller leans in conspiratorially. "Alright, this one is *really* like a movie plot," they promise. "Imagine a lonely aristocrat with a fabulous fortune and not a single person he cares about…" The tale is introduced like a dark fairy tale: Once upon a time in Portugal, Luis Carlos de Noronha Cabral da Camara – a nobleman with a name longer than the line outside a Louis Vuitton sample sale – had no close family or friends to leave his wealth to. So what did he do? In a move that had *all* of Lisbon scratching their heads, he walked into a notary's office, grabbed a phone book, and randomly picked 70 total strangers to be his heirs. Yes, completely random – he literally said "that one, and maybe this one…" to *seventy* names, like a morbid lottery draw. When he died in 2007, these unsuspecting people started receiving letters from a lawyer informing them that a *mysterious benefactor* had left them a fortune. Most thought it was a scam or a cruel prank – after all, who expects to inherit from a man you've never even heard of? One 70-year-old heiress, on being told she'd inherited from Luis, said *"I thought it was some kind of cruel joke… I'd never heard of the man"*. (Frankly, it *does* sound like those spam emails: "You have won an inheritance, dear friend, send your bank details." Only this time it was *real* and the bank actually *sent* money.)

Random will beneficiaries … it's the only time being in the phone book truly paid off. In 2007, Portuguese aristocrat Luis Carlos shocked 70 strangers by naming them heirs to his estate. Each stranger got a letter about their unexpected windfall, prompting reactions from disbelief to joy.

As details emerged, the story only got more intriguing. Luis Carlos, despite his impressive lineage, was reportedly an unhappy soul – an illegitimate son of aristocracy, few friends, no children. He had inherited some real estate and cash, and indulged in expensive hobbies like motorcycles, target shooting, and copious drinking (clearly living the *"live fast, die unpredictably"* philosophy). By the time he drafted his will about two decades before his death, he must have decided that none of his distant relatives (or the tax man) deserved a dime. He explicitly wanted to avoid his estate going to the state, which he felt had already taxed him to death (literally). Perhaps, in a final act of port-soaked whimsy, he thought, *"I'll show them – I'll give it all away to strangers! That'll confuse everyone."* An old friend speculated that Luis *"wanted to create confusion by leaving his things to strangers".* If so, *mission accomplished.* The result was a real-life lottery: 70 ordinary people woke up one morning as heirs to a share of a nobleman's fortune. It wasn't millions each – his estate included a 12-room Lisbon apartment, a country house, a luxury car, healthy bank accounts and a couple of motorbikes, to be divided 70 ways. Still, each lucky stranger walked away with several thousand euros, at least. Not exactly a Bezos-level bonanza, but imagine getting *any* sum out of the blue because your name happened to be in a phone book. It's the stuff of daydreams: a twist of fate that makes you part of a telenovela you never auditioned for.

At our brunch, this story triggers a flurry of analogies. "It's like Willy Wonka's golden tickets, but with inheritances!" one friend exclaims. Another suggests, "Or like Oprah going, *You get a house!* and *You get a motorbike!* to random people – except Oprah usually knows her audience." Indeed, it's as if Oprah had decided to bequeath her riches not to her loyal staff or godchildren, but to 70 names from the Yellow Pages just to keep things interesting. Even Donald Trump gets dragged into the banter: "Imagine if Trump randomly left Mar-a-Lago to some guy named Juan Gomez he picked out of a Miami phone book – the chaos would melt the internet." We howl at the absurdity. Yet, Luis Carlos's story isn't just a punchline; it carries a peculiar poignancy. It underscores how *absurd human vanity* and isolation can become. He had wealth and pedigree, but apparently no trust or love for anyone close – so he made a statement by scattering his assets to the wind. It's loneliness immortalized in a will. You might say he took *"distribution of assets"* to anarchic new heights. If there's a lesson from his tale, perhaps it's a bittersweet one: nurture real connections in life, or else risk your legacy being literally *phonebook random*. As our storyteller notes wryly, "Better to choose your heirs around the dinner table than by flipping through the directory." We all clink glasses to that nugget of wisdom.

2.4 Roses from Beyond the Grave

By now, our sides ache from laughing and our minds are reeling from the sheer audacity of these last laugh wills. We've heard of revenge served cold, fortunes gone to the dogs, and lotto-style legacies. It's only fitting to end on a sweeter note – a palate cleanser in this rich diet of absurdity.

The storyteller, ever the show person, saves the most heartwarming tale for last. "Not every outrageous will is bitter," they announce, eyes twinkling. "Some are disarmingly romantic. This one always gets me — and it's absolutely true." The table leans in, perhaps expecting a ghost or a scandal. Instead, we get Jack Benny, the legendary American comedian, and a final wish that could thaw even the most jaded L.A. hearts.

When Jack Benny died in 1974, he left behind a comedic legacy — and one extraordinarily tender provision in his will. For decades, Jack had joked on stage about being cheap (his comic persona was famously penny-pinching). But in private life, he adored his wife, Mary Livingstone, with whom he shared 47 years of marriage. In his will, Jack arranged for a simple yet profoundly touching gift: every single day after his death, Mary would receive one long-stemmed red rose delivered to her door. And indeed, the day after Jack's funeral, a florist showed up at Mary's house with a red rose and kept coming *every day* thereafter. Mary, initially perplexed by the daily bloom, eventually learned the truth: Jack had pre-paid and instructed this daily delivery for the rest of her life. *"One red rose to be delivered to me every day for the rest of my life,"* Mary recounted, describing Jack's final act of love. It was as if he'd said, "My love, I may be gone, but I'll still make you smile every morning with a fresh rose." If this doesn't make you misty-eyed (or at least goosebumped), you might need a top-up of that mimosa.

A single red rose — the ultimate symbol of enduring love. Comedian Jack Benny's will instructed that a long-stemmed red rose be sent to his wife Mary every day after his death. For the rest of her life, Mary received daily roses, a gesture that turned a comedic icon into a posthumous romantic legend.

In a chapter filled with spite and oddities, the power of thoughtful love shines bright in Jack Benny's story. It's proof that not all wealthy folks use their wills to settle scores or one-up their frenemies. Some use them to send a love letter that transcends even the grave. Our brunch group lets out a collective "aww," an oasis of sincerity amid our laughter. We picture Mary Benny finding each morning's rose on her doorstep, a reminder that she was cherished. One of us jokes that this was the longest-running "delivery subscription" ever – beating Amazon Prime by a mile – and infinitely more romantic. Another quips that Taylor Swift could write a song about this level of devotion (perhaps a sequel to "Love Story" with a legal twist). Jack Benny essentially gave us a real-life fairy tale epilogue: *Happily Ever After*, one rose at a time. It's a family lesson in love and loyalty, showing that sometimes the grandest gesture is also the simplest.

As the brunch winds down, the storyteller raises their glass for a final toast. We've journeyed through a gallery of humanity at its most *extra*: a poet's sly revenge, a lawyer's deranged legacy, a billionaire's dog-obsessed whim, an aristocrat's random generosity, and a comedian's enduring love note. What do we take away (besides the urge to triple-check our own grandparents' wills for hidden surprises)? Perhaps it's this: Wills are the last messages we send to the living, and those messages can be as twisted or as tender as the lives that shaped them. We've seen *the pettiness of revenge from beyond*, where ego and hurt drove men like Heine and Zink to get the last laugh (or last groan) in death. We've witnessed *the absurdity of human vanity*, in Helmsley's indulgence and Luis Carlos's theatrical randomness, reminding us that great wealth can amplify our quirks into full-on crazy. And in Jack Benny's rose, we've felt *the power of thoughtful love*, a reminder that a loving heart can find a way to remain present, even in absence.

In the end, these stories are absurd and hilarious, yes, but also illuminating. They're absurd family secrets shared over wine and finger sandwiches, the kind that make you shake your head and promise yourself to leave a *sensible* will (maybe with a joke or two, but nothing that requires a court intervention). They teach us about vanity, vengeance, and affection in the strangest of contexts. As we clink glasses one last time, someone notes with a grin: "If there's a moral here, it's to live so your will doesn't have to do *stand-up comedy* at your family's expense." Or, as another laughs, "Maybe just leave roses, not conditions." Cheers to that – and may we all be lucky enough to inherit laughter and love rather than spite and Trouble (pun intended). The brunch fades out with giggles and reflective smiles, each of us secretly resolving to keep our own *fortune and folly* in check long before any lawyer gets involved in writing it down.

Chapter 3

The Heist of a Lifetime – Thieves, Cons, and Final Reveals

3.1 "I Am D.B. Cooper"

Few names spark as much intrigue as D.B. Cooper – the mysterious skyjacker who leapt from a plane in 1971 with $200,000 strapped to his body and vanished into legend. For decades, the world obsessed over Who was D.B. Cooper? This airborne outlaw became a folk hero of sorts, inspiring everything from movies to meme-worthy Marvel cameos (yes, even *Loki* joked that he was Cooper mid-prank). The FBI chased hundreds of leads, armchair detectives traded wild theories on Reddit, and every so often a new suspect's name made headlines. Yet the real Cooper remained as elusive as a Snapchat filter at a senior center. Then, in 1995, a 70-year-old man named Duane L. Weber dropped a bombshell on his deathbed: "I'm Dan Cooper," he whispered to his wife Jo. In that moment, a lifetime of myth suddenly took a very personal turn for one bewildered widow.

Jo Weber initially had no clue what "Dan Cooper" meant – she thought her dying hubby might be babbling nonsense. But in the months after Duane's death, Jo became Nancy Drew with a pension. Eerie clues from their life together began clicking into place, turning her living room into a scene from *National Treasure* – minus Nicolas Cage's hairpiece. She remembered Duane having nightmares in which he muttered about "leaving fingerprints on a plane" and waking up in cold sweats. He once casually pointed out a knee injury he claimed came from "jumping out of a plane" (cue raised eyebrows). Most damning of all, Jo found a library book about the Cooper case with Duane's own handwriting scribbled in the margins – like a student obsessively studying for the ultimate crime exam. It was as if her mild-mannered husband had lived a double life as America's most wanted sky pirate.

- **Midnight mumblings:** Duane thrashed in his sleep about *"fingerprints on a plane"*, as if reliving a heist. Not your average sweet dream, unless your spouse is secretly D.B. Cooper.

- **Mysterious injuries:** He carried an old knee injury and offhandedly said it came from *"jumping out of a plane."* At the time, Jo likely rolled her eyes – sure, and this scar on my arm is from wrestling Bigfoot.

- **Incriminating literature:** A library book on D.B. Cooper had Duane's notes all over it. Talk about *highlighting* the evidence – apparently the man couldn't resist adding an *annotated bibliography* to his own crime.

Jo Weber went to the FBI with her suspicions, essentially saying, *"Honey, I think I married Cooper."* The Bureau took a hard look at Duane Weber. He was a World War II veteran with a 20-year rap sheet of burglary and forgery – a man quite comfortable on the wrong side of the law. On paper, he fit the Cooper profile: military experience, criminal tendencies, even a passing resemblance to the composite sketch (slick hair, and a penchant for dark sunglasses – very *Men in Black* chic). For a while, Duane Weber *was* one of the more compelling suspects in the unsolved NORJAK case (FBI-speak for the Northwest Orient Airlines hijacking). Jo Weber even became a minor celebrity in the D.B. Cooper subculture, passionately telling anyone who'd listen that the love of her life was the daredevil hijacker who got away.

Yet in the grand tradition of this confounding case, even a deathbed confession didn't close the file. The FBI eventually reported that fingerprints and DNA from the hijacked plane did not match Duane Weber. In other words, if he *was* D.B. Cooper, he somehow managed not to leave the same prints or genetic traces – a trick even Houdini would envy. Skeptics pointed out that over the years *dozens* of people have claimed to be D.B. Cooper (so often that it's practically a cliché: old men whispering dramatic confessions like *"It was me, see? And no one ever even knew!"* while twirling imaginary mustaches). One tongue-in-cheek report noted that if every confession were true, Flight 305 would have been standing room only with skyjackers. The Cooper saga has more wannabe culprits than an Agatha Christie novel.

So was Duane Weber truly the man who pulled off the ballsiest mid-air heist in U.S. history? The mystery endures. Jo Weber remained convinced until her own passing that her husband and Cooper were one and the same, and many in the public remain tantalized by the possibility. After all, Duane's confession gave a human face (and a widow's heartbreak) to a legend. It's hard not to root for at least *one* ending to this story – for the ordinary grandpa in Florida to indeed have been the dashing thief who said "Take the money and dive." On the flip side, maybe Duane was just seeking one last thrill, claiming the Cooper crown for himself as a kind of grand finale to his life of crime. In a case built on myth, even the *confession* might have been a final con.

Either way, the cultural impact of D.B. Cooper is undeniable. He's become an almost Robin Hood-esque figure (minus, you know, actually giving to the poor) – a symbol of sticking it to "The Man" and vanishing into the night. People tell their kids campfire stories about him, artists write songs, TV shows reference him for a quick nostalgia pop. Cooper represents the allure of *getting away with it*, the ultimate unsolved mystery. And perhaps there's a strange family lesson in Duane Weber's tale for the rest of us: sometimes the person you've shared your life with has *another life* entirely that you never knew about. Grandma Jo learned that in jaw-dropping fashion. It makes you wonder what secrets that quiet uncle or neighbor down the street might be harboring. Not that everyone's hiding a felonious past, of course – but if a beloved husband could secretly be a legendary outlaw, it does give a whole new meaning to "my better half." The D.B. Cooper obsession speaks to our enduring fascination with secrets, trust, and the ultimate question of *how well do we really know our loved ones?* And until the day the mystery is definitively solved (don't hold your breath), D.B. Cooper – whoever he was – will remain a ghost hovering in our collective imagination, winking from the clouds, forever unattained and unmasked.

3.2 The Great Bank Robber Next Door

On a summer Friday in 1969, Theodore "Ted" Conrad strolled into his Cleveland bank job like it was any other workday – sharp 20-year-old kid, probably humming a Beatles tune under his breath. By closing time, he nonchalantly stuffed a paper bag with $215,000 in cash (worth over $1.7 million today!) and walked out the door as if heading for a lazy weekend. It sounds like the climax of a Hollywood film – and in fact it *was* directly inspired by one. Ted was *obsessed* with the Steve McQueen movie *The Thomas Crown Affair*, in which a bored millionaire pulls off a bank heist for kicks. He watched it half a dozen times, bragging to friends that robbing his own bank would be a piece of cake. In a case of life imitating art, Ted basically said "Hold my beer, Steve McQueen" and went for it. By the time his coworkers noticed the money was missing on Monday, Conrad had a two-day head start on the law. The legend of Cleveland's slickest bank thief was born – but the story was far from over. In fact, it was just beginning its strangest chapter: the one where the notorious criminal becomes your super nice suburban neighbor who hosts BBQs on July 4th.

For 52 years, Ted Conrad lived in plain sight under a new identity, evading one of the longest manhunts in U.S. history. He didn't flee to Brazil or hole up in the wilderness like some criminal on the lam – nope, Ted pulled a *Kansas City shuffle*. He moved to the Boston suburbs, changed his name to Thomas Randele, and proceeded to live what looked like the most *boringly normal American life* imaginable. Think about the audacity here: the guy pulls off Ohio's biggest bank heist, then essentially says,

"Time to play house." Under the alias Thomas Randele, he became a golf pro at a country club, selling luxury cars on the side. He wore polos and baseball caps, waved to the neighbors, and even donated to local police charities for good measure. (The irony! The thief was funding the cops' donut brunch, possibly chuckling to himself every time he wrote a check.) He also binge-watched crime shows like *NCIS* and *Unsolved Mysteries* – imagine sitting next to him as *America's Most Wanted* features *his* case, and he just casually sips his lemonade. Talk about nerve. Ted had effectively written, directed, and starred in his own long con, a real-life *Breaking Bad* in reverse: the criminal who breaks good and becomes the beloved family man, all while hiding a loot-filled past.

Ted – now Tom – got married, had a daughter (Ashley), and by all accounts was a doting dad and devoted husband. Ashley grew up thinking her father was an ordinary gentle soul who grilled burgers, took her to school, and asked after every home-cooked meal, *"So, can I make this again?"* (He was apparently a pretty good cook, who knew?). In a delicious twist of fate, Thomas Randele even befriended local law enforcement as a genial community member. Picture it: the head of the neighborhood watch is secretly a fugitive bank robber. It's like an *Andy Griffith Show* episode directed by Quentin Tarantino. Suburban life has always been about keeping up appearances, but Tom took keeping up appearances to Ocean's Eleven levels of commitment.

Of course, the FBI and U.S. Marshals *never* forgot Ted Conrad. He was featured on true-crime shows; generations of lawmen chased leads across the country. His case became the stuff of Ohio legend – parents would quip "eat your veggies or D.B. Cooper and Ted Conrad will get you!" (Okay, maybe not, but he was notorious). Over the decades, investigators came close a few times but Ted was clever. He'd forged documents to build his new identity, effectively erasing Ted and birthing Tom. In fact, a U.S. Marshal on the case later noted that when people lie about who they are, they often keep the lie **"close to home."** Indeed, "Thomas Randele" wasn't randomly plucked; it echoed *Thomas Crown*, his favorite movie character, almost like an Easter egg he left for sleuths.

So how did the jig finally end up being up? Fifty-two years after the heist, in 2021, Tom Randele was dying of lung cancer and decided to confess his secret to his family. It's the kind of confession you'd expect to come with a dramatic musical score – Ashley (now an adult) learns that her dear old dad *was* the infamous Ted Conrad, the very man she'd heard whispers about in local lore. Mind. Blown. To their credit, the Randele family kept the secret even as Tom passed away in May 2021. But fate – and forensic paperwork – intervened. Investigators had been piecing together clues, matching old documents of Conrad's to recent records of Randele's (a 2014 bankruptcy filing, for example). Tom's obituary provided key details too: his birth date, place of birth, and parents' names aligned with Ted's. The Marshals showed up in Boston, likely half in awe that this grandpa had outfoxed them for so long. In November 2021, they publicly revealed the truth: the mystery of Ted Conrad was solved. Conrad and Randele were one and the same. The *Great Bank Robber Next Door* had been unmasked at last – albeit too late to slap cuffs on him. Once again, our man was a step ahead, escaping justice by way of mortality.

For the investigators – notably Deputy U.S. Marshal Peter Elliott – this was a moment of bittersweet triumph. Peter's own father, John Elliott, had hunted Conrad in the 1960s and never gave up. The elder Elliott lived in the same neighborhood as Ted back then, talk about close to home! Though John passed in 2020, his son solved the case a year later, bringing a touching family legacy full circle. Peter said he hoped his dad was "resting easier" knowing this decades-long mystery was finally laid to rest. It's almost poetic – two families, the Conrads and the Elliotts, unknowingly entwined in this long dance of lies and truth for half a century.

So what's the takeaway from good old Ted/Tom's tale? First off, it proves that truth really can be stranger than fiction – if you pitched a script where a 20-year-old steals a fortune and becomes a model citizen in suburbia for 50 years, Hollywood execs might say "Nah, too unrealistic." Yet here we are. Family lessons? Well, think about Tom's wife and daughter: they adored a man who turned out to have a dark secret. That could breed cynicism (*was their entire life a lie?*), but it can also teach forgiveness and understanding – that people can change, that someone can do a bad thing in their youth and spend the rest of their life making up for it. By all accounts, Tom was a loving husband and father; perhaps that was his way of atoning. There's also a cautionary nugget: you might *think* you know your family, but sometimes you're living with a chapter from a true-crime bestseller sleeping on the couch. Lastly, Ted's story shows the weight of long-term deceit. Imagine carrying that secret every day, worried a speeding ticket or a nosy neighbor could unravel everything. It must have been a relief, in a way, to finally tell his family the truth before he died. In our era of constant oversharing, Ted Conrad's half-century secret stands out – reminding us that sometimes the quiet neighbor has the loudest story. And if you ever suspect your parent might be a fugitive... maybe check the garage for 50-year-old cash bundles, just in case.

3.3 The $30 Million Museum Heist

In the annals of art crime, some thieves steal paintings or jewels – but Na'aman Diller stole *time* itself. Specifically, he yoinked 106 antique clocks and watches from a Jerusalem museum in 1983, including a gold pocket watch crafted for Marie Antoinette valued at over $30 million. Yes, you read that right: a single watch worth more than a yacht full of Bitcoins. This wasn't some smash-and-grab by a petty crook; it was a Spider-Man-style burglary executed with meticulous precision and a dash of Hollywood flair. Diller, a notorious Israeli burglar with a flair for the dramatic, had cased the L.A. Mayer Museum for Islamic Art and discovered its security weaknesses – notably a broken alarm and some complacent guards (perhaps too busy debating soccer scores). One night, he struck: bending iron bars on a back window with a special tool, crawling through with a rope ladder, and masking his movements by parking a car out front as a decoy. You can almost picture him in a black turtleneck, doing the Mission: Impossible dangling trick over glass display cases of priceless clocks. In a matter of hours, Diller had pulled off Israel's costliest heist ever, snatching timepieces not just of huge monetary worth but immense historical value. The crown jewel was the legendary Marie Antoinette watch by Breguet – known as the *"Mona Lisa of the clock world*". How do you fence something so famous? Simple: you don't. Instead, Diller embarked on a lifelong love affair with his ill-gotten treasures, a secret sojourn that blurred the line between romance and felony.

Diller didn't steal those clocks to get rich quick – in fact, he barely sold any of them. To the investigators who later unraveled the case, it seemed he did it for "the thrill of it," to achieve an "incredible feat" just for bragging rights in his own diary. Imagine the mindset: he wasn't raiding a museum to fund a lavish lifestyle (he already had plenty of other burglaries and even a famous bank tunnel heist under his belt). No, this was personal – like an art lover collecting masterpieces, except the gallery was his secret stash spread across continents. Diller carefully stashed the stolen clocks in safes and safe-deposit boxes around the world: Tel Aviv, Munich, Basel, Paris, Los Angeles – a global scavenger hunt only he knew about. In some twisted way, it's almost romantic: the thief couldn't bear to part with the beautiful objects he stole. He preserved them like a dragon guarding its hoard. Police later found he kept detailed, almost tender notes about each clock's components and condition, scrawled on anything from scraps of paper to toilet paper. (Yes, toilet paper – he literally gave a crap about these clocks!) One detective quipped that *luckily* for the museum, Diller was so passionate he maintained each piece in pristine condition, as if he were their clandestine curator. It's a bizarre thought: while curators fretted for 25 years, the thief himself was gently winding the stolen clocks in secret, ensuring time still ticked smoothly in his hidden troves.

And what about Mrs. Diller? Enter Nili Shamrat, the wife who eventually became the unexpected hero(ine) of this saga. Nili had dated Diller in the 1970s, moved to the U.S., then reconnected and married him in 2003, just as he was dying of cancer. Only then, it appears, did Na'aman Diller finally spill the beans about his decades-old heist, in a dramatic deathbed confession worthy of a telenovela: *"Honey, by the way, I stole like a hundred clocks... and I'm leaving them to you."* Indeed, Diller left the stolen collection to his wife in his will, alongside, presumably, instructions on where to find all those caches of ticking contraband. One imagines Nili's mixed emotions: *My dying husband did WHAT?* – part outrage, part incredulous awe. After Diller's death in 2004, she quietly tried to monetize some of the clocks. In 2006, the museum curators got an anonymous offer: pay $40,000 and a few of your missing clocks can return home. The museum bit, recovering 40 pieces including the Marie Antoinette watch (steal a $30M watch, sell it back for $40k – Diller clearly wasn't in it for profit!). This secretive buyback tipped off Israeli police, who traced the seller back to Nili Shamrat. When they showed up at her Los Angeles home in 2008, it must have felt like a time-traveling SWAT team appearing from the 1980s. Sure enough, they found even more clocks hidden on the premises, and Nili confessed that her late husband had told her everything. The great clock caper was finally solved.

Even the detectives couldn't help a bit of professional admiration for Diller's artistry. "He was a legendary robber – very different, very intelligent, unique style," said one investigator, practically tipping his hat to the deceased thief. They learned that Diller's cunning went even further: he had been an immediate suspect back in '83, but they dismissed him because his passport showed he wasn't in the country then. Turns out, he forged his alibi as expertly as he picked locks. The man literally stole time and then faked time – doctoring dates to throw police off. It's the kind of detail that cements his legacy among the pantheon of great con artists.

But for all the cinematic cool, let's not forget the *human* side of this heist. Those clocks weren't just dollar signs; they were pieces of history cherished by the museum's founder and staff. When they vanished, it was a gut punch – imagine working to preserve cultural heritage and overnight it's gone, poof. The collection's founder, Vera Salomons, had assembled those timepieces out of love for art and history. Diller's actions stole more than objects – he stole time in the poetic sense: years of public enjoyment and scholarship that could have been. It's fitting then that after the truth came out, most of the clocks were returned to the museum, restored to their rightful place in the halls (albeit decades late). Time, as they say, heals all wounds – and in this case, *timepieces* healed some too.

From a family perspective, the Diller caper is a doozy. Nili Shamrat found out she was married to the "Time Bandit" only at the very end. That's a heavy legacy to inherit – literally, she inherited talismans of her spouse's secret life. To her credit, she cooperated with authorities to recover the treasures (after initially trying the hush-hush sale route). One can draw a lesson about legacy and love here: do we truly know our partners? Diller kept Nili in the dark for years, arguably to protect her, or perhaps because the secret was part of his identity he wasn't ready to surrender. It was only when faced with mortality that he let her in on it – effectively handing off his burden. In a way, it became *her* story too, and she helped close it. Their relationship had spanned continents and decades, and ended with a confession that tested the limits of loyalty. Imagine discovering the love of your life was both a romantic and a felon, that every anniversary clock he gifted you might have been literally stolen! Nili's experience shows that loving someone often means inheriting their secrets – and deciding what to do with them. In her case, she chose to right some of his wrongs, even as she benefited a bit (the museum's $40k payoff) before coming clean. The fine line between romance and felony indeed: Diller's passion for horology (and maybe a dash of kleptomania) became an odd kind of love letter to his wife – a treasure bequest that was both a blessing and a curse.

In the end, the $30 Million Museum Heist is a story of time lost and time regained. It's got everything: a cat-burglar with *Lupin*-like ingenuity, a trove of dazzling antiques hidden like Easter eggs around the world, a widow turned accomplice-after-the-fact, and a resolution that brought precious artifacts back home. Perhaps it reminds us that even when time is stolen, truth has a way of *clocking in.* The past catches up, and even the most brilliant thieves can't escape the ticking clock forever. So next time you hear a clock chime, think of Na'aman Diller – somewhere, in that great beyond, he's hopefully realized that while he briefly owned Time, in the end, Time owned him.

3.4 The Golden Submarine Hoax

If you've ever fallen for a clickbait headline or a Photoshopped meme, don't feel too bad – people have been getting duped by fake images for *ages*. Case in point: the Loch Ness Monster's most famous photo, known as the "Surgeon's Photograph." For six decades, this grainy black-and-white snapshot of a long-necked creature in the Scottish lake was held up as *the* proof that Nessie was more than just a whiskey-fueled hallucination. Taken in 1934 and published in the *Daily Mail*, it showed a serpentine head and neck rising from the water, creating ripples that fueled a million fantasies. The photographer was listed as Colonel Robert Wilson – a respectable British surgeon who claimed he was just enjoying a drive when, *by Jove*, he saw something and snapped a pic. His reluctance to be associated with it (he didn't want his name used, hence "surgeon's photo") only added to the mystique. And boy, did the world buy it. For decades, most people accepted the image as genuine evidence of Nessie's existence. Sure, a few skeptics pointed out the "monster" looked kinda *small* (one analysis in 1984 argued the object in the photo was only 2–3 feet long, not exactly the 30-foot plesiosaur of legend). But believers waved that off – after all, seeing is believing, right? In the pre-Photoshop era, a photograph was gospel truth to the public. The Loch Ness hype became a tourism boon and a cultural phenomenon. Nessie was on postcards, in movies, heck, *the* Nessie was basically the Bigfoot of the Highlands, with this photo as her glamorous headshot.

Then came 1994, the year truth finally stood up in the boat and yelled, *"Gotcha!"* It turned out the monster was nothing more than a golden submarine – or rather, a toy submarine with a fake monster head attached. The perpetrator of this grand hoax? A man named Christian Spurling, who at age 90 decided to clear his conscience (perhaps figuring he didn't want to meet St. Peter with a Loch Ness lie on his ledger). Spurling confessed that the famous photo was an elaborate hoax. And not just any hoax – it was a family affair and an act of revenge rolled into one. Spurling was the stepson of Marmaduke Wetherell, a big-game hunter who had been publicly humiliated by the *Daily Mail* a year before the photo. See, in 1933 the *Mail* hired Wetherell to find Nessie. He came back with plaster casts of huge footprints by the lake – which turned out to be made with a dried hippo's foot (Victorian pranksters had a weird sense of humor, using umbrella-stand feet). The newspaper made Wetherell look like a fool who fell for a prank, and he was furious. So Wetherell cooked up a scheme to hoax the very media that had hoaxed him. Talk about *revenge of the nerds*, cryptozoology edition.

Spurling's deathbed confession spilled the whole tea: In 1934, Wetherell had Spurling, a skilled model-maker, build a miniature monster – basically a Loch Ness critter head and neck crafted from wood putty. They affixed it to a toy submarine bought from Woolworth's – the *golden submarine* of legend (okay, it was likely painted grey, but let's give it a regal hue for flair). Wetherell's son, Ian, helped stage the shot. The crew took their model to the loch and carefully placed it in the water, angling for a realistic photograph. At one point, a water bailiff (like a lake ranger) approached, nearly spoiling the fun, so they sank the model submarine with a swift kick, sending Nessie to a watery grave (it presumably still lies somewhere in Loch Ness muck to this day). To sell the hoax, they needed a frontman with credibility – enter Colonel Wilson, who was a friend of a friend and enjoyed a good practical joke. Wilson agreed to be the "photographer" of record, lending the photo an air of respectable British stiff-upper-lip authenticity. He turned in the plates to be developed and handed the impressive one to the *Daily Mail*. On April 21, 1934, the paper splashed the now-iconic image under headlines basically shouting "Monster of Loch Ness Captured on Film!" The world went nuts. Wetherell no doubt had a good chuckle seeing the *Mail* trumpet the very monster he faked, after they'd made him a laughingstock. It was the ultimate troll – 1930s style.

For 60 years this hoax held strong. Generations of wide-eyed kids and credulous adults were enthralled. Sure, experts squinted and pointed out inconsistencies (the ripples looked small, as if the object was miniature – which it was). But the mythos around Loch Ness was so strong, fueled by earlier sightings and a human *desire to believe* in something fantastical, that the hoax was practically canon. It wasn't until Spurling's confession and investigative work by researchers in the 1990s that the truth fully surfaced. In fact, a 1975 article had already alleged the photo was fake, but it didn't get wide attention. Spurling's admission in the 90s was the clincher. As one report succinctly put it: *"In 1994, 60 years after it graced the pages of the Daily Mail, Christian Spurling verified the photograph as a hoax by admitting his involvement."* Marmaduke Wetherell, the mastermind, had died decades earlier, never fully vindicated in public – but perhaps privately satisfied that he pulled one over the press. The *Surgeon's Photo* went from holy relic to punchline: the *Daily Mail* had been out-pranked by a toy submarine and a guy named Marmaduke.

The impact of this revelation was profound and a little bittersweet. On one hand, skeptics felt vindicated: *See, we told you it was a fake!* On the other hand, a lot of folks who grew up with Nessie in their imagination had to swallow the jagged little pill that their beloved monster might be, well, a myth after all. It's as if Santa's elf came forward and said "actually, we faked the North Pole photos." Even though rationally most knew the photo was iffy, that tiny hope that *maybe* Nessie was real took a hit. However, Loch Ness tourism didn't die – people still come hoping for a glimpse of something, because legends have a life of their own. And Nessie had other (less credible) photos and sonar blips to keep believers believing. Interestingly, the hoax's exposure also served as a teachable moment in critical thinking and media literacy. It remains an "important part of photo history and serves as a reminder of photography's fickle relationship with truth". In other words, just because there's a photo doesn't mean it's real – a mantra that in the age of deepfakes and AI-generated images is even more relevant. The Surgeon's Photo was basically the 1930s equivalent of a viral fake on Twitter. It taught us to question what we see, ask who benefits from us believing it, and consider how even very smart people (doctors, newspaper editors, scientists) can be fooled by a *cleverly crafted image* that confirms what they *want* to believe.

Fast forward to today, and the Golden Submarine Hoax feels almost charming in its simplicity. No complex CGI, no Photoshop – just a toy, some clay, and a keen sense of showmanship. Compared to modern internet hoaxes – which can involve massive coordinated lies or digital manipulation – there's something quaint about the Loch Ness prank. It was essentially a meme that went analog-viral, transmitted by newspapers and word of mouth rather than retweets and likes. And like many viral sensations, its originators remained anonymous until much later, watching their creation take on a life of its own. One can't help but appreciate the showmanship: Wetherell and Spurling gave the world a myth that endured for most of a century.

From a cultural perspective, the Loch Ness hoax underscores our collective yearning for wonder. People *wanted* to believe in Nessie – just as many want to believe in UFOs, Bigfoot, or the Chupacabra. A good hoax doesn't work unless it taps into some hope or fear in society. During the 1930s, with the Depression on, perhaps a fantastical creature in a remote Scottish lake was an exciting diversion. Today's hoaxes (think fake celebrity news or conspiracy theories) similarly play on desires and anxieties. The Loch Ness pranksters didn't have Facebook to spread their mischief, but they understood the media of their time and human psychology. The lesson is equal parts humility and humor: humility in that we humans can be fooled pretty easily when we *want* something to be true, and humor in that, well, sometimes we just have to laugh at how gullible we can be. Wetherell didn't get rich off the hoax; his reward was seeing the dupers duped. And ultimately, when Spurling's confession came out, most people greeted it with a chuckle and a shrug. Nessie's photo being fake didn't kill the legend – it merely shifted it. Now the story of how the world was fooled became part of Loch Ness lore.

In family terms, there's even a quirky little lesson: the hoax was a collaboration between a stepfather and stepson (and other friends). It's almost heartwarming, if you ignore the deceit – a multi-generational bonding project! So maybe the family takeaway is that shared creative endeavors, even naughty ones, can bring folks closer. Perhaps in the Spurling/Wetherell household, pulling the world's leg was their version of a father-son fishing trip. Would I recommend hoaxing the planet with your Grandpa? Probably not – but I bet their family dinners were never boring. In the end, the Golden Submarine Hoax left us with an enduring fable about truth: it might be down there in the dark depths, or it might be a painted toy – and it reminds us to always keep a healthy skepticism, even while we chase monsters.

3.5 The One Big Lie – Bernie Madoff's Confession

When it comes to real-life confession-based scams, it's hard to top the sheer audacity and fallout of Bernie Madoff – a man who was once the *wizard of Wall Street* but turned out to be operating behind a curtain of deceit. Madoff wasn't a princess (and certainly not charming), but for decades he was treated like financial royalty, trusted with the fortunes of celebrities, charities, and thousands of ordinary folks. He curated an image of a genius investor and philanthropist, serving as chairman of NASDAQ and rubbing elbows with the elite. People literally begged him to take their money. Little did they know, Bernie's golden touch was as real as Rumpelstiltskin – he was spinning lies into an empire of *phony wealth*. For at least 20 years (possibly longer), Madoff ran the largest Ponzi scheme in history, a house of cards that grew to an astonishing $65 *billion* in paper value. He promised steady, impressive returns and delivered them – but only by secretly using new investors' money to pay off earlier investors, classic Ponzi style. It was, as he later confessed, "one big lie" from start to finish.

The crazy part is how long he got away with it. Madoff was the ultimate con artist in a designer suit – he exploited not greed so much as *trust* and image. He created a "front of respectability and generosity," wowing people with his charitable donations and impeccable credentials. He groomed investors like a seasoned Svengali: some he enticed by exclusivity (his fund was *invitation-only*, making having a Madoff account feel like joining a secret club of the chosen few), others he lulled by consistency (his returns were not absurdly high, just reliably good, 10-12% a year, which somehow made it more believable than a wild 50% spike). Many victims were affluent and financially savvy on paper – but they trusted Bernie because everyone else did. It became an emperor's new clothes scenario; red flags were rationalized away. A few brave whistleblowers, like financial analyst Harry Markopolos, waved their arms for years saying "Guys, these numbers don't add up!" – but regulators failed to act until it was too late. Bernie cultivated that trust masterfully: he served as a NASDAQ chairman, advised the SEC on regulations (oh, the irony), and was known for his *chummy country club demeanor*. He even swindled nonprofits and charities – about 10% of the money he stole was from charitable organizations, showing that no target was off-limits, not even causes for the public good. Talk about *stealing candy from a benevolent baby*.

Finally, in December 2008, with the global financial crisis in full swing, the walls closed in. Too many investors requested withdrawals as the economy tanked, and Madoff didn't have the money to pay them (since, surprise, it was never really invested). Facing a tidal wave of redemptions he couldn't fulfill, Bernie Madoff confessed to his sons that his entire asset management business was a fraud – a giant Ponzi scheme that was collapsing. He told them it was all "one big lie," effectively admitting he'd been faking it all along. This was no gentle end-of-life confessional delivered in a rocking chair – it was a panicked admission to family in the midst of a crisis. His sons, Mark and Andrew, who had worked in the legitimate side of his firm, were reportedly stunned (they claim they had no idea). They did something heart-wrenching but necessary: they turned their father in to the authorities the very next day. Can you imagine the turmoil of that moment? One day you're proud of Dad's success; the next he tells you he's the greatest con man of our era, and you're on the phone with the FBI. That's Greek tragedy level family drama right there.

When news of Madoff's confession and arrest hit, it was an explosion in the financial world. Investors who once toasted to their quarterly statements suddenly realized those profits were fictitious. Charities discovered their endowments were vapor. The ripple effect was catastrophic: people's life savings gone, foundations crippled, even a few suicides resulted from the losses and shame. Tragically, one of those was Madoff's own elder son, Mark, who took his life exactly two years after his father's arrest. Mark couldn't escape the shadow of the scandal and the accusatory whispers (some suspected the sons *must* have known; official investigations, however, did not charge them, and they maintained innocence). Madoff's younger son, Andrew, died of cancer in

51

2014 – he too said the stress likely contributed to his illness. Bernie effectively imploded his own family with his lies: his wife Ruth, who once enjoyed a life of luxury, was left ostracized and reportedly living modestly, having cut ties to the man she'd spent over 50 years with. In an almost darkly comedic footnote, Ruth claims when Bernie first confessed to her, she had to ask *"What's a Ponzi scheme?"*. Imagine learning over dinner that your husband was a fraud on a scale you can barely even spell. The Madoff clan name, once respected, became synonymous with deceit and betrayal.

Now, Bernie's story might not have the same *ha-ha* humor as a Loch Ness prank or a golf-pro-turned-robber reveal, but there is a satirical edge in the absurdity of it all. He basically played the entire financial system like a grand piano. He was the *Forrest Gump* of finance gone wrong – present at all these illustrious moments, shaking hands with regulators, donating to charities, all while swiping everyone's wallets. In one interview from prison, Bernie even had the gall to partially blame the victims' greed, saying everyone wanted to believe in him because they were making money and chose to ignore the warning signs. That's like the Big Bad Wolf saying those pigs practically *asked* to have their houses blown down. It's infuriating – but it also exposes a truth about scams: they often exploit our hopes and blind spots.

So, what lessons do we glean from the Madoff saga (aside from "don't give your money to dudes who guarantee the moon")? First, it underscores the importance of skepticism and due diligence. If something is too consistently good to be true, maybe peek behind the curtain. Even sophisticated investors failed to do that with Madoff – they were dazzled by the aura. In a sense, Bernie was running a long con not unlike Ted Conrad's double life, but on a massive scale: he hid in plain sight under the veneer of respectability. He leveraged personal relationships and the *"special club"* vibe to make people feel *grateful* to invest with him. This is Cult Psychology 101 and Ponzi 101 rolled into one.

Second, on a family level, Madoff's confession saga is a Shakespearean tragedy. The man may have spared his sons from legal culpability by telling them the truth (and thus allowing them to report it), but in doing so he crushed them emotionally. Imagine the person you looked up to most turning out to be a villain. It's an enduring lesson that our actions echo through our loved ones' lives. Bernie's "one big lie" not only incarcerated him (150-year sentence, essentially a life term) but cursed his family name and arguably contributed to his son's death by suicide. No amount of ill-gotten wealth could ever be worth that price.

And yet, there's a strange catharsis in Madoff's fall. The final reveal – him being led away in handcuffs, admitting guilt in court in 2009 to *11 felonies* – was like a morality play for the world. In an era where so many powerful people seem to escape consequences, here was one who did not. He was publicly shamed, stripped of assets, and left to rot in prison (where he died in 2021). It doesn't return the money, but there was *justice* of a sort.

Humor in the Madoff tale comes mostly from the absurd contrasts: the idea of this "kindly Uncle Bernie" figure who volunteered at charities, while literally robbing those charities blind. It's like discovering Mr. Rogers was running a meth lab in the Neighborhood. People who visited Madoff's office recall how unimpressive it was – a small, nondescript setup – and how his inner sanctum of fraud was just a 17th-floor office where he and a few loyal lieutenants cranked out fake account statements. It wasn't even high-tech; they used an old IBM computer to forge documents. The emperor had no clothes, and not even a fancy tailor. In the end, Madoff's confession came not from a pang of conscience but from imminent collapse – he essentially said, *"I couldn't keep up the act, so I turned myself in."* He even told the judge at sentencing that he started the scheme in the early '90s and at first thought he could extricate himself quickly but "I just couldn't". As if he got *talked into it* by... who? The devil on his shoulder? The audacity! It's almost comedic that he floated the idea he was a victim of circumstance in his own con. The judge and everyone else did not buy that line – he alone chose to keep doubling down for decades.

So, if we package a family lesson from the Madoff debacle, it might be this: honesty and integrity matter, because their absence can destroy those closest to you. All the yachts and mansions in the world can't replace your family's trust once it's broken. Bernie's wife and sons presumably loved him deeply; by all accounts he was a caring father prior to the reveal. But once the truth emerged, that family was fractured beyond repair. Ruth Madoff made a point of saying her "integrity means everything" as she denied knowing about the scheme – it shows how even she, perhaps innocent of the crime, felt tainted by association.

And in a larger sense, Madoff's confession is a cautionary tale about unchecked ambition and deception. It invites a bit of satirical comparison: Bernie was like a real-life Emperor Palpatine of finance – seemingly a benign senator (finance elder) who was actually a Sith Lord zapping the accounts of the Republic, until Darth Vader (the market crash) threw him down the shaft. Or maybe he's more of a Gollum, ensnared by the "Precious" (other people's money) until it consumed him. In any case, his story, though devoid of the lightheartedness of our other heists and hoaxes, serves as the final reveal in our chapter: a reminder that truth does out, and when it does, it can be both devastating and liberating. Devastating for those who built their lives on lies, yet liberating for those lies to end.

In a conversational sense: We can almost imagine Bernie in his prison cell reflecting, *"I made off with billions (pardon the pun), but lost everything that truly mattered."* The man whose surname literally sounds like "made-off" did indeed make off with fortunes, only to confess and lose it all. If that isn't poetic justice, I don't know what is. So as we close the book on these thieves, cons, and final reveals, remember the wise words often misattributed to the Bible but true nonetheless: *"Be sure your sin will find you out."* Whether you're claiming to be D.B. Cooper, hiding stolen clocks in your attic, faking a lake monster, or juggling ledger entries on Wall Street – eventually, the truth catches up. And when it does, oh boy, what a story to tell. Just pray that your family can survive the telling.

Chapter 4

Till Death Do Us Part... Twice – Bigamy, Betrayal, and Double Families

4.1 The Spy with Four Wives

Alexander Wilson and his first wife Gladys on their wedding day in 1916. Little did Gladys know her MI6 spy husband would go on to marry three more women without ever divorcing her.

In the annals of secret families, few capers top the real-life spy saga of Alexander "Alec" Wilson. An English novelist and wartime MI6 officer, Wilson didn't just lead a double life – he led a quadruple life. Over several decades, he maintained four separate wives (plus assorted children) in utmost secrecy. If that sounds like the plot of a far-fetched thriller, well, it *was* – Wilson himself wrote successful spy novels, all while writing elaborate fiction in his personal life. He spun lies as deftly as a novelist, telling each wife he was away on "secret missions" when he was really hopping between families like a clandestine polygamist. Imagine James Bond settling down with Miss Moneypenny *and* three other Mrs. Bonds on different continents – that's the kind of absurd spy trope we're dealing with here, minus the Aston Martin. Wilson essentially made domestic *bigamy* his ultimate espionage stunt.

How on earth did he pull it off? For starters, he never divorced any of the wives, sidestepping legal alarms by tweaking his identity each time.

In fact, each marriage certificate sported a different middle name for him – a sly trick to avoid detection. One could say he took his talent for creating cover identities a bit too literally. His first and only legal marriage was to Gladys Kellaway in 1916 (they had three children together). By the mid-1920s, while posted abroad, this roguish spy embarked on a new romance with Dorothy Wick on a voyage to India. He married Dorothy around 1928 under an alias, fathering a son with her. Wife #2 and their child believed Wilson died heroically on a WWII mission in 1942 – a tall tale he himself concocted before ghosting them. (Yes, he literally faked his death to one family. Cold War, meet cold-hearted.)

Not content with two secret households, Wilson next wooed a young secretary, Alison McKelvie, in London in 1940. They fell in love amidst the Blitz, married, and had two sons. Alison was about 30 years his junior, and she knew he'd been married before – but she had no idea he was *still* married to the others. Whenever he vanished for "intelligence work," Alison's suspicion grew that he might be up to something else. Little did she know, her suave spy-hubby was spending those long "MI6 trips" playing husband and father in his other homes. By the mid-1950s, incredibly, Wilson added a fourth wife to his roster: he bigamously wed a nurse named Elizabeth Hill and had another son. The audacity is jaw-dropping – four wives in different locales, seven children in total, and never once coming clean. He was essentially living out a farcical crossover of *Mission: Impossible* and *Mad Men*, juggling identities and anniversaries like a plate spinner. (One wonders if he had a color-coded calendar or just a really good memory for alibis.)

For a man ostensibly devoted to Queen and Country, Wilson sure had a funny way of interpreting "For Queen and Country" at home. His spy career provided the perfect cover for deceit. As an MI6 agent, he had clearance to live in the shadows – and boy, did he use it. He told elaborate lies about top-secret postings and even staged a fake burglary at one point to gain sympathy. When real spy work dried up (he was dismissed from MI6 amidst some scandals), he kept lying about covert ops to explain his lengthy absences. It's as if he blurred the line between fiction and reality: by day, writing adventure novels and translating intercepted cables; by night (and weekends), criss-crossing between families. No wonder the BBC turned his tale into a juicy drama called *"Mrs. Wilson."* In that miniseries, actress Ruth Wilson actually portrays her own grandmother Alison Wilson – a meta twist, since Ruth is Alexander's real-life granddaughter. Talk about family therapy through art! The show captures the moment in 1963 when Alison's world shattered: upon Alexander's sudden death, she discovered she wasn't his only Mrs. Wilson. In real life, Alison found hidden letters that revealed her "late" husband had never divorced Gladys, wife #1, and even had children by her. Imagine the scene: you're grieving your spouse, only to unearth evidence that he had a whole secret clan calling him husband and Dad. It's the kind of revelation that makes you question every date night and love letter – *was he really in Cairo on MI6 business, or celebrating Christmas with Wife #2?* Alison must have felt like she married a stranger, because in many ways she had.

The full scope of Wilson's double-(triple-quadruple?) life didn't come to light until decades later. Astonishingly, it was as late as 2005 that historians and journalists helped piece together Alexander's sprawling family jigsaw. His various children, by then grown and gray-haired themselves, had lived oblivious of one another's existence. When the truth finally emerged, it led to an extraordinary family reunion: in 2007, all of Wilson's surviving offspring met in person for the first time. Picture that meeting – siblings and half-siblings ranging in age from their 50s to 80s, exchanging bewildered looks and photo albums, bonding over the shared absurdity of their fathers' lies. It's a poignant reminder that while Wilson succeeded in keeping his secret through his life, the consequences unfolded long after he was gone. The emotional fallout was complicated. There was shock, betrayal, even a sense of dark humor (one of Wilson's grandchildren quipped that the whole saga was "one way to grow the family tree"). Alison herself, rather than go public, quietly wrote a memoir for her sons about her experiences, to be opened when they were grown. She likely hoped to impart some understanding of the man she loved – or thought she knew.

Spy fiction tropes indeed ran wild in Wilson's real story: false identities, secret dossiers (those letters!), and a web of lies worthy of a John le Carré novel. But unlike James Bond, who neatly ties up his missions in a couple of hours, Alexander Wilson left a messy legacy that took half a century to untangle. His tale carries a sobering family lesson beneath the satire: living a lie can fracture lives in unimaginable ways. The truth, as delayed as it was, did come out – and the healing only began when it did. As one commentator noted, Wilson "married four times without ever divorcing" – essentially maintaining *several lives all at once*. It's a feat of deception that is more bewildering than admirable. Ultimately, his wives and children were denied the truth for years, which is its own tragedy (albeit one wrapped in a cloak-and-dagger comedy of errors). The *Mrs. Wilson* drama and subsequent research gave the families clarity and a chance to connect the dots he left scattered.

In a bizarre way, Alexander Wilson's story is both a cautionary tale and a dark comedy. Cautionary, because it shows the utter unsustainability of such deceit – even a trained spy couldn't keep it airtight forever. And darkly comedic, because, honestly, you almost expect a Monty Python sketch: "No one expects the Spanish Inquisition – or the fourth wife!" The man managed to say "till death do us part" four times over and technically never parted until his own death. He was the spy with four wives, and when his number was finally up, the truth exploded his carefully constructed fiction. Family secrets, like time bombs, have a way of detonating eventually. In Wilson's case, the blast radius spanned generations. If there's any silver lining, it's that his children, once strangers, found siblings they never knew and forged relationships from the wreckage. Still, one imagines Thanksgiving (or rather, Christmas) dinner would've been *awfully* awkward had all Mrs. Wilsons and their broods ever sat around the same table. Alexander Wilson lived on the edge in both espionage and marriage; ultimately, he paid the price posthumously, with his loved ones left to pick up the pieces. As a wry epilogue, his granddaughter Ruth – armed with the truth – told the story to the world on screen, ensuring that fact proved stranger than spy fiction in the end.

4.2 The Two-Family Funeral Fiasco

Funerals are usually solemn affairs – unless, of course, the deceased managed to double-book his life. One Midwestern family got the shock of a lifetime when a beloved husband and father passed away, only to have a second wife and her children show up unexpectedly at his funeral. If there's a textbook definition of "awkward," this was it. Mourners on one side of the chapel noticed unfamiliar faces on the other, and murmurs spread: *Who are those people crying by the casket?* The answer landed like a grenade: they were *his other family*. It turned out this ordinary-looking suburban dad had led a secret parallel life for years. He had two households in different towns, each blissfully unaware of the other – until that fateful funeral brought them under one roof. Picture the scene: two grieving widows, each thinking *she* was the only Mrs., each with kids who had no idea they had half-siblings standing across the aisle. It's the kind of plot twist that would make a soap opera writer blush. In fact, the whole debacle felt like a cross between a Jerry Springer episode and a daytime telenovela, except nobody had the presence of mind to shout "Jerry! Jerry!" in the funeral home. (Though one imagines the whispered conversations among stunned relatives had a similar vibe.)

Initially, the mood swung from sorrow to confusion to outright turmoil. One widow (let's call her Wife A) looked at the other (Wife B) in disbelief: *"I'm his wife."* Wife B, clutching a tissue, responded, *"I'm his wife!"* – a real-life Spider-Man pointing meme, but with marriage licenses. The emotional chaos that followed was by all accounts intense. "It was a huge shock, and it messed up everyone involved," one family friend recounted later. Both sets of children had their entire history rewritten in a moment. Every memory of Dad was now suspect – was he *really* away on business all those times, or visiting the *other* family? The betrayal cut deep. Some relatives were angry at the deceased for his deception (hard to confront him about it now, given the circumstances), while others directed anger at the "other" family, as if they were intruders – even though they were victims of the lie as well. Small-town Midwestern communities aren't known for scandal, so you can imagine the local gossip mill working overtime. One can picture church ladies whispering over coffee: *"Did you hear about Bob? Two wives! Two entire sets of kids! Bless their hearts..."* The cultural fallout was significant. This wasn't a cosmopolitan big city tale of double lives; it was happening in heartland America, where family values run deep and bigamy is about as welcome as a tornado at a picnic.

In the immediate aftermath, grief was compounded by confusion. The funeral service itself turned into an impromptu family meeting of strangers. There were not one but *two* eulogies – each wife attempting to sum up "her" husband's life, while processing the realization that his story had an extra chapter she never knew. (One can only imagine the grim humor of those eulogies: "He was a loving husband, a devoted father..." – at which point Wife A and Wife B lock eyes like, *seriously?*) If it weren't so heartbreaking, it could have been a dark comedy sketch. At the reception, instead of just casseroles and condolences, there were furious whispers and a lot of *meaningful* side-eye. The poor funeral director probably needed a stiff drink after refereeing that scene.

With time, the dust settled – somewhat. The two families had to figure out the practicalities (death certificates, wills, who gets what – the law does not look kindly on bigamy, so untangling the estate must have been a legal circus). More importantly, they had to navigate the human side of this tangle. The half-siblings, who literally met over their father's coffin, had a choice: either retreat to their separate corners, or attempt to build a bridge out of this bizarre revelation. In this true case, a bit of both happened. Years later, some healing occurred: the man's son from Family A became close with the daughter from Family B, forging a genuine sibling bond. A few of the kids managed to develop a relationship, finding solace in shared memories of their complicated dad. They realized *they* were blameless in this and actually had a lot in common (genetically and otherwise). There's a bittersweet image of them perhaps meeting up occasionally, comparing childhood photos of the same dad at two birthday parties in two different houses, or joking darkly that their father was like a traveling salesman cliché on steroids. These half-siblings chose connection over the continued drama, illustrating that family can sometimes blossom in the unlikeliest soil. However, not everyone found peace: the first wife and her other children "never really got over it and pretend [the second family] doesn't exist" even years later. Denial can be easier than facing the hurt, especially when pride and public embarrassment are at play. Who could blame them? In one fell swoop, their husband/father's legacy went from cherished family man to punchline of the town. It's a tall order to forgive and forget.

From a wider lens, this funeral fiasco holds some universal lessons (delivered with a side of gallows humor). For one: secrets eventually surface, often at the most inconvenient times. You might carry on a double life for years, but all it takes is one slip – or an unexpected tragedy – for truth to burst out of the coffin (literally, in this case). It's a testament to the saying "What's done in the dark will be brought to the light." In our digital age of DNA tests and Facebook, secret families are harder to keep hidden; yet even decades ago, as in this story, fate found a way to unveil the subterfuge. Another takeaway: the resilience (and strangeness) of family dynamics. When the unthinkable happens, families either pull together or fall apart – here we saw a bit of both. Some relationships broke permanently, while others bent and reformed into something new.

And we can't ignore the psychological aspect: what drives a person to lead such a duplicitous existence? Was this bigamist husband a sociopath, a thrill-seeker, just profoundly selfish? Perhaps he rationalized that he truly loved both families. (One imagines him compartmentalizing his life so completely that he became two different people in his own head.) It's telling that none of his loved ones had a clue; he must have been alarmingly good at lying. A friend of the family noted how no one knew anything; it was a huge shock that messed everyone up. The man's ability to deceive was, in a twisted way, almost impressive – like watching a magician's long con – except the final trick sawed his loved ones in half. In the wreckage, those left behind had to make sense of their identities. The wives likely questioned whether their marriages were ever "real." The kids had to reconcile the father they adored with the fraud he perpetrated. It's a lot to unpack in therapy.

Culturally, we often see bigamy played for laughs in movies or treated as rare sensational news. But for the people in this story, it was painfully real. If there's a humorous angle (and we *are* trying to keep a witty tone here), it might be this: the situation is so outrageous that it forces a nervous chuckle. I mean, meeting surprise siblings at a funeral – you couldn't script a darker comedy. It's like an episode of *This Is Us* written by a cynic: tragic, ironic, and forcing everyone to redefine what "family" means. One could reference the old *Spider-Man* adage, "with great power comes great responsibility," except in this case, *with great duplicity comes great dysfunction.* Our Midwestern bigamist likely never imagined both worlds colliding, but when they did, he unwittingly left behind an example of what *not* to do in family life. Honesty, as tough as it may be, could have spared a lot of people a world of hurt (and one incredibly tense funeral).

In the end, this two-family funeral fiasco stands as a jaw-dropping illustration of betrayal. It shows that while love and affection may have existed genuinely in each family, the deceit undermined it all. The story lives on in family lore – told perhaps with a grim laugh years later: "Remember when we met our half-siblings? Ah, yes, at Dad's funeral – surprise!" The humor is not lost, but neither is the pain. Yet the fact that some of the siblings chose to become family in the aftermath is a hopeful epilogue. They refused to be defined solely by their father's sins. Family, once the truth is out, can take many forms. In this case it took the form of two shattered families tentatively merging into one, over the memory of a man who vowed "till death do us part" to two women at once. Death did part him – and then united his deceived loved ones in the most unintended way. Talk about *resting in pieces*.

4.3 The Newsman's Double Life

Charles Kuralt was the kind of figure Americans invited into their homes every Sunday morning – a genial, trusted TV newsman with a folksy charm. He was famous for his "On the Road" segments on CBS, traveling the country to spotlight heartwarming stories of everyday people. With his soft voice and avuncular presence, Kuralt seemed like the last person who'd harbor a scandal. And yet, behind that Rockwellian public image, he carried on a hidden life that could have been lifted from a novel. For 29 years, Kuralt maintained a secret relationship with another woman, managing a delicate two-world balancing act that astonished even those who knew him. By day, he was the devoted family man and celebrated journalist; by stealth, he was the doting companion to his long-time mistress, Pat Shannon, in Montana. In a way, he lived his own double-feature: one reel wholesome Americana, one reel private passion. It wasn't until he passed away in 1997 that the full story spilled into public view, revealing an extraordinary double life.

The outlines of Kuralt's secret are jaw-dropping. Starting in the late 1960s, he met Patricia "Pat" Shannon, a divorced schoolteacher, and began a relationship that would span almost three decades. All the while, Kuralt was married – first to his wife Sory (whom he divorced in 1982), and then to his second wife Suzanna "Petie" Kuralt, whom he remained married to until his death. Petie and the rest of the world had no inkling that Charles's heart (and considerable time) were divided for so long. To keep things under wraps, Kuralt cleverly used his job as cover. After all, he was literally on the road hundreds of days a year, crisscrossing America to film TV segments. Who would question if he took a few extra "travel days" here and there? It was the perfect alibi. And so he built a second life out West: he and Pat shared a love of nature and solitude in rural Montana. Kuralt bought property along the Big Hole River – a scenic 90-acre retreat – where he and Pat spent idyllic days fly-fishing, camping, and even celebrating Christmases together. He quietly paid college tuition for Pat's kids, helped support her financially, and even purchased her a cottage in Ireland. In effect, he was running a shadow household on the other side of the country, complete with all the trappings of commitment except one: no legal marriage, and absolute secrecy. Friends who saw Kuralt with Pat in Montana just assumed she was an old friend; colleagues at CBS were none the wiser. Kuralt *excelled* at keeping up appearances – so much so that even his wife Petie didn't know he and Pat owned land together or had any relationship at all until after he died. That's how airtight his compartmentalization was.

The secret finally unraveled thanks to a letter – a dramatic twist fit for a TV movie. In June 1997, lying in a New York hospital and sensing the end was near, Kuralt penned a heartfelt letter to Pat. "Something is terribly wrong with me," he wrote, adding that he would have his lawyers ensure she inherited the remaining acreage of their Montana paradise "if it comes to that". He mailed this letter shortly before he died on July 4, 1997. After his death, Pat produced the letter, claiming it as evidence that Charles wanted her to have the land. What followed was a courtroom confrontation between two women Kuralt hoped would never meet – his widow Petie (and later his children from his first marriage) versus Pat, the secret companion. The very existence of this legal battle meant that Kuralt's private life suddenly became headline news. Imagine the public's surprise: the roving reporter known for feel-good stories had been writing a rather sensational story of his own off camera. The press dubbed it a "double life" and they weren't exaggerating. Court documents later confirmed that Kuralt and Pat had a secret relationship for 29 years. For nearly three decades, he moved between two worlds – "one with a wife and career on the East Coast, another with a woman clear across the country" as the Washington Post described it. The revelation cast Kuralt's famous sign-off line, "On the road again…," in an entirely new light – he was on the road again, and again, living out two separate existences.

The estate fight itself was poignant and a bit surreal. Pat argued that the letter should count as a holographic will leaving her the 90-acre Montana property, since it clearly expressed Charles's intent. Kuralt's family initially balked, suggesting the letter was merely a promise to change the will later, not a legally binding bequest. Over two years of legal wrangling, more details of the secret affair emerged. We learned, for instance, that Charles had already quietly deeded Pat 20 acres and a cabin during his lifetime (masquerading the gift as a "sale" by providing her the money). He had been planning to transfer the remaining 90 acres in a similar under-the-table way before he fell ill. These aren't the actions of a casual fling; they're the kind of long-term arrangements you'd associate with a committed second partnership. Eventually, a Montana judge ruled in Pat's favor in 2000, declaring the letter valid and awarding her the land.

By then, Petie Kuralt had passed away as well (she died in 1999), and it was Charles's adult daughters who opposed Pat's claim. When the decision came down, Pat, then in her 60s, simply expressed hope that "wounds could begin to be healed" and that they could all remember Charles fondly. It was a gracious statement after such a tumultuous ordeal.

The juxtaposition of Kuralt's public persona with his private reality is striking. Here was a man celebrated for his authenticity and appreciation of simple, honest lives – yet he was hiding a profound deception from those closest to him. It's not that Kuralt was exposed as some kind of villain; by most accounts he truly cared for both his wife and Pat, and was generous and loving in both relationships. But one can't help noting the irony: a journalist who told other people's true stories never told the full truth of his own. His colleagues were flabbergasted. Many admitted that in hindsight, the clues were there (Kuralt's frequent "fishing trips" to Montana, for example), but no one put it together. This was pre-social media and pre-TMZ, a time when a famous figure's private life could indeed remain opaque if carefully managed. Kuralt managed it masterfully – albeit at great moral cost.

From a family perspective, the fallout was likely complex emotionally. Petie Kuralt, by all reports, died never knowing the extent of her husband's second life (perhaps a mercy for her). Kuralt's daughters, however, had to grapple not only with losing their father, but losing the image they had of him. That's a heavy double whammy: grief intertwined with a sense of betrayal. Yet, interestingly, this scandal did not utterly tarnish Kuralt's legacy in the public eye. Perhaps because it emerged after his death, many fans shrugged it off as a very human failing of an otherwise beloved figure. In the pantheon of public figures with secret mistresses, Kuralt's case was almost old-fashioned and oddly tender – no salacious tell-alls or tabloid fodder beyond the estate case. Pat herself even wrote a memoir titled *"Charles and Me,"* shedding light on their relationship with a tone of love rather than scandal. She painted a picture of a man who divided his time and affection, not out of malice, but because he had built deep bonds in two places and couldn't bear to break either. It doesn't excuse the deception, but it humanizes it. Life isn't always tidy, and Kuralt's was messier than anyone guessed.

From a witty angle, one might say Kuralt took the concept of "Work-Life balance" to an extreme: he had Work-Life A and Work-Life B. Or that he truly embodied the phrase "on the road" – as in on the road to see Wife, then on the road to see Mistress, rinse and repeat. It's almost remarkable how he kept all the threads untangled for so long. If a lesser man tried that, he'd likely mix up names or addresses at some point ("Hello darling – er, I mean, *other* darling…"). Kuralt, consummate storyteller, kept his narrative straight. One can't help but draw parallels to other famous double-lifers. He was no international man of mystery like Alexander Wilson with four wives (Kuralt had the decency to stick to one extra partner, not three!), but in the realm of media figures, he stands out. It's as if Mr. Rogers had a secret family in another state – the cognitive dissonance is that strong. In Kuralt's case, his "On the Road" persona vs. off-the-road reality provided a rich contrast. On camera, he emphasized honesty, decency, and the beauty of everyday life. Off camera, he orchestrated an elaborate deception that lasted until his final breath.

What's the family lesson here? Perhaps that even good people are capable of compartmentalizing in astonishing ways, and that secrecy can be born not only from malice but sometimes misguided love or fear of hurting others. Kuralt likely thought he was sparing feelings by keeping things secret – not realizing that secrets have a way of hurting people *more* when they inevitably emerge. It's also a lesson about the complexity of human relationships. His wife Petie and Pat Shannon were two very different women who each made him happy in different ways. One provided stability and partnership in his public life, the other gave him escape and solace in a wild refuge where he wasn't the TV star, just Charles. It's sadly poetic: he had to split himself to achieve what he thought was fullness of life. The result was that neither woman got 100% of him, and after he was gone, they were left with legal papers and an epitaph that had an asterisk.

Yet, Kuralt's story isn't viewed with the same harshness society might reserve for, say, a politician caught in lies. Perhaps because his contributions – those warm-hearted stories – still resonate, and no one he loved intended to vilify him after death. In fact, Pat only went to court to get what she was promised; she never dragged his name through the mud. The dignity with which both sides handled it (publicly at least) is noteworthy. In a final twist of fate, Kuralt's letter did become his last will for Pat, and she got to keep the place that had meant so much to them.

One might say *justice* was served, or maybe *karma* – depending on your view.

In a humorous sense, one could imagine Kuralt in the afterlife giving a characteristically gentle narration of his own saga: "As it turns out, I had one more American story to tell – mine – and it was a doozy." Indeed, the tale of Charles Kuralt's double life reminds us that the private corners of people's lives can hold great surprises. It adds a layer of complexity to the legacy of a man who, until then, was seen as almost entirely wholesome. The takeaway? Heroes have their flaws, and even the man who brought us stories of others had a secret chapter in his own story. It doesn't erase the good he did, but it certainly keeps us talking – and perhaps shaking our heads, half in disbelief, half in rueful amusement – about the lengths to which one can go to live two lives in parallel.

4.4 The 92-Year Secret Affair

You'd think after 70 years of marriage, a couple would have no surprises left. By their 90s, most pairs are content with gentle routines – a morning espresso, a stroll to the piazza, perhaps lovingly arguing over the correct way to cook pasta. Not so for one Italian couple, who proved that marital drama has no expiration date. In a bizarre late-life bombshell, a 92-year-old Italian husband decided to *come clean* about a secret he'd kept for decades: he confessed to his 96-year-old wife that he'd engaged in a long-running affair years earlier. This wasn't a fleeting indiscretion either, but a 13-year liaison he had carefully hidden. One imagines him clearing his throat at the dinner table and saying, "Cara, there's something I need to tell you..." What followed was not the gentle reconciliation one might pray for in old age, but a full-blown decision to divorce – *in their 90s!* Yes, after seven decades and a soccer team's worth of kids and grandkids, this nonagenarian duo headed to splitsville, cementing their place in history as perhaps the oldest couple ever to call it quits.

The story made headlines worldwide, partly because of the ages involved and partly because, well, it's just *astounding*. The husband – let's call him Antonio – had apparently been wracked by guilt or perhaps influenced by an urge to set things right before the Grim Reaper came knocking. The wife – we'll call her Rosa – was utterly blindsided. Imagine her perspective: at 96 years old, having spent your entire adult life with this man, you suddenly learn that for over a decade (maybe back when he was in his spry 70s or 80s!) he was romantically involved with someone else. It's the kind of revelation that could give a person a heart attack – except Rosa's heart, fueled by equal parts sorrow and Italian fury, proved exceptionally strong. Legend has it she demanded a divorce on the spot. And frankly, who could blame her? "Till death do us part" had been the promise, but *he* apparently treated it as "till temptation do us part (for 13 years)." Rosa wasn't about to let that slide, not even in the ninth inning of life.

News reports at the time (this happened around 2011) identified the couple only by first names and initials due to privacy, but the Italian press had a field day. Some wryly pointed to the couple's fiery southern Italian blood as the catalyst for such an explosive breakup in extreme old age. (Antonio was originally from Sardinia, Rosa from Naples, a pairing of passionate temperaments if ever there was one.) Indeed, there's something operatic about the whole affair (pun intended). It's like a Puccini opera where the final act suddenly fast-forwards to the characters as nonagenarians airing ancient infidelities. One imagines neighbors peering over balconies as Antonio moved out with his belongings – a few suits, a walking cane, perhaps the TV – while muttering, "Mamma mia, at their age!"

The absurdity and humor in this situation are undeniable. For starters, the notion of a 99-year-old man (Antonio hit 99 by the time court papers were filed) furiously scrawling "Divorzio!" on legal forms is something you'd expect from a satire, not reality. The world's media gleefully noted that the pair would become the world's oldest divorcees once proceedings finalized, snatching the title from a British couple aged 98 who divorced a few years prior. (Perhaps there's a Guinness World Record certificate in this somewhere, hopefully written in extra-large font.) And while divorce is usually a solemn matter, it's hard not to chuckle at the timing. I mean, 77 years of marriage down the drain because of a fling that happened when Truman was President? Talk about holding a grudge – or conversely, about the *importance of trust at any age*. Depending on your point of view, either Antonio should have kept that secret to his grave, or Rosa should have let bygones be bygones considering, you know, the whole *mortality* thing looming. But humans are humans, whether 19 or 99, and betrayal cuts deep. Rosa's reaction was basically, "Better to die alone than with a cheat." It's oddly empowering – a statement that it's never too late to stand up for yourself, even if your standing is a little wobbly with a walker.

Let's fill in a few factual details for context. According to reports (and it's famously documented in court records), Antonio found some old letters in a drawer around Christmastime that tipped him off to Rosa's past affair – oh yes, plot twist: some accounts suggest it was Rosa who had the affair back in the 1940s, and Antonio discovered her secret correspondences. In that version, he confronted her, and she admitted she had been unfaithful about 60 years earlier for a brief period. Antonio, rather than shrug it off as ancient history, decided it was an unforgivable breach. He literally marched down to the courthouse in early January and filed for divorce from his 96-year-old wife. The narrative we're expanding here had flipped the genders – with the 92-year-old husband confessing *his* affair – but either way, the end result is the same: an almost-century-old marriage imploded by infidelity revealed in the final chapter. In both scenarios, it's clear the couple had weathered plenty of storms (including *World War II*, for heaven's sake), yet this was the storm that sunk the ship. As one article quipped, apparently Antonio had never heard of "let bygones be bygones". Indeed, bygones my foot – not when pride and heartbreak were on the line.

The couple had a large family: five children, a dozen grandkids, and even great-grandchildren. One can only imagine the faces of those kids when Nonno and Nonna announced they were splitting. At first, some grandchildren reportedly thought it was a joke or a symptom of cognitive decline: "Surely Grandpa is confused; maybe he thinks he's divorcing Grandma in a dream?" But no, Antonio was deadly serious. When asked why now, he supposedly said he just couldn't bear the thought of this secret going unresolved – that it "gnawed at him" from the inside.

Psychologists might say he was seeking *closure*, even if it blew everything apart. Rosa, once confronted (whether by evidence or confession), apparently tried to persuade him to reconsider – I mean, splitting assets and moving at almost 100 years old isn't exactly convenient. But Antonio was resolute. One might humorously say that after 70-odd years of matrimony, he was *done* and wanted his remaining time solo, thank you very much.

The deeper lesson here (yes, there is one beyond the farce) touches on honesty, forgiveness, and the weight of secrets. It's easy to say, "Good grief, why not just let it lie? At that age what's the point?" But clearly, to Antonio (and to Rosa if we reverse the roles), the principle mattered even more than practicalities. It's a testament to how trust is timeless – it doesn't matter if you're 22 or 92, finding out you've been betrayed hurts just the same. In fact, in some ways it might hurt more after a lifetime together because that partnership is a huge part of your identity. Suddenly, the narrative of "we made it through everything" is shattered. The absurdity is that there was hardly any "life after divorce" to be had – it's not like either was about to start a new family or hop on Tinder (perish the thought). Yet, perhaps for both, it was about ending the story on *their own terms*. Antonio likely did not want to play the forgiving fool; Rosa might have felt she deserved better than a philanderer husband even for a year. Or maybe, just maybe, there's a dark comedy in wanting to be right even when it's nearly irrelevant. "I'll show you – I'll divorce you!" "Fine, go ahead!" It's like the final spike of drama they could muster, a last hurrah of passion in a twisted way.

The public, of course, found the whole thing morbidly fascinating. This wasn't a celebrity split or a billionaire bust-up; these were ordinary people in the twilight of their lives revealing that even then, *life can surprise you*. It's a reminder that people in their 90s aren't just sitting around playing bingo – they have inner worlds, secrets, old resentments, and yes, sometimes even the energy to start over. After the story broke, there were reports that both found some peace separately. Antonio allegedly moved in with one of his sons (no, not with a 30-years-younger mistress as some cheeky outlets speculated – by all indications, the affair he revealed had ended long ago). Rosa, for her part, lived out her remaining years with support from their daughters. Whether they ever spoke again isn't known. One hopes perhaps they found forgiveness at the very end. But given the Italian press's commentary about fiery temperaments, they probably remained stubborn to the grave. In an Italian divorce, nobody typically "stays friends" – and certainly not at nearly 100 years old!

From a humorous standpoint, this tale illustrates that marriage can indeed be a lifelong battlefield – with skirmishes even in extra innings. You can picture the couple's guardian angels facepalming and saying, "Seriously, you two? At this age?" It also underscores a comedic truth: no matter how old we get, we're never completely removed from the follies of love and pride. The same emotions that drive 20-somethings to storm out after a cheating revelation drove a 99-year-old to a courthouse. Perhaps it's oddly comforting that some things – the importance of trust and the sting of betrayal – are truly ageless.

So, what's the deeper lesson in this nonagenarian soap opera? Perhaps it's "honesty is the best policy"... but maybe time your honesty a bit better. If Antonio had found a way to discuss this 50 years earlier, maybe they'd have had time to heal. Or if Rosa had fessed up (if we go by the original scenario where she strayed), perhaps they'd have confronted it when they were younger and more flexible (physically and emotionally). Alternatively, one might conclude that some secrets, if you've kept them for 60 years, might as well remain secrets – why detonate the bomb when the clock is winding down? But then again, Antonio's conscience couldn't let him rest. In a darkly humorous twist, telling the truth did set him free – just not in the way one usually expects. It set him free of his marriage, and it set Rosa free of her illusions.

Finally, there's an underlying sweet sadness here. This couple shared 70 years of memories: raising children, going through life's ups and downs, likely celebrating countless birthdays and anniversaries. They almost made it "till death," only to have *trust* – or the lack of it – pry them apart at the very end. One could argue that divorcing at that stage is more symbolic than practical, a final assertion of self-respect. Rosa essentially said, "I will not let my last years be a lie." That is both heart-breaking and oddly admirable. And Antonio, whether confessing or reacting, said, "I cannot die with this secret on my chest," which is a human impulse we see often – people unburdening themselves when time grows short. It just so happened his truth was the kind that blows up a family album.

In the annals of extraordinary breakups, the tale of the 92-year-old secret affair stands out for its mix of humor and pathos. It teaches us that people don't magically become saints with age – they remain complicated, passionate, and sometimes ridiculous creatures to the end. If you ever visit Italy and hear locals gossip about "the almost-100-year-old divorce," you'll know it's this story. They'll shake their heads and chuckle, perhaps clinking a glass of wine: *Salute* – to love, to life, and to whatever crazy thing comes next, no matter how late in the game. After all, as this couple proved, it's not over till it's over… and even then, it might end with a dramatic flourish. Till death do us part? Not quite – in their case, it was *"till an old secret do us part."* And that's a family lesson for the ages.

Chapter 5

Sins of the Father – Illicit Children and Family Secrets

5.1 The Segregationist's Secret Daughter

Imagine a fire-and-brimstone segregationist preaching about the evils of racial mixing by day, and secretly tucking in his biracial daughter by night. Sounds like a plot twist from a satire about the Jim Crow South, right? Well, real life beat the satirists to it. Senator Strom Thurmond of South Carolina – famous for thundering that black and white should never mingle – had in fact *already* mingled quite personally with his family's 16-year-old African American maid. The result? A baby girl named Essie Mae Washington-Williams, a secret living rebuttal to all of Thurmond's public rhetoric. It's as if the universe saw this man drawing a strict color line and decided to give him a daughter who could walk right across it.

For decades, Essie Mae was a ghost in Thurmond's closet, known only to a few and hidden from the world like a scandalous photo in a locked drawer. Thurmond, ever the Southern gentleman hypocrite, quietly supported his secret daughter financially through college while publicly championing segregation. Picture him signing anti-integration manifestos with one hand, while sending discreet checks to his integrated offspring with the other. The situation oozed irony so thick you could drizzle it over grits. It remained under wraps for nearly 70 years – a testament to just how tightly one can cling to a lie when a political career is on the line.

The big reveal finally came in 2003, but not until after the 100-year-old Thurmond had taken his final bow (and by bow, we mean he literally exited stage left from life). Essie Mae, by then in her late 70s herself, stepped forward and said, "Surprise! That arch-segregationist was my dad." Cue the collective gasp. It was the ultimate "Maury Povich" moment, except Maury wasn't needed because the proof was in old letters, payments, and, well, her very existence. One can only imagine the Twitter frenzy if it had happened today – #SecretDaughter would be trending, and Thurmond's ghost would be furiously facepalming. Perhaps the most astonishing part: Thurmond's *legitimate* (and white) children publicly acknowledged Essie Mae as their sister, essentially confirming the truth.

For comedians and commentators, it was the kind of irony you couldn't script better. The man who spent a lifetime railing against race mixing turned out to have mixed his own genes in the most personal way. Late-night talk show hosts likely pinched themselves – how often does a setup this perfect fall into your monologue? Thurmond basically became a posthumous punchline, proving that even a century-old politician can still surprise everyone from beyond the grave. It's not every day you see a family photo updated to include the half-sibling who had been there all along in the shadows.

In hindsight, Thurmond's saga offers a painfully comedic lesson in the absurdity of prejudice and the futility of buried secrets. Here was a man shouting from the rooftops about purity and separation, all while his own gene pool was integrated like a homemade smoothie. The next time a public figure vehemently denies something, remember old Strom – the man who filibustered civil rights for a record 24 hours, yet couldn't escape a family reunion with the very diversity he opposed. Life has a wicked sense of humor, and karma, it seems, sometimes takes the form of a long-lost daughter tapping you on the shoulder – or on your gravestone – to say "Howdy, Dad."

5.2 Parisian Double Life

Now let's hop across the pond to a tale that feels ripped from a French romantic dramedy. François Mitterrand, the two-term President of France, managed to run an entire country and a secret family on the side like he was auditioning for a juicy Netflix series. To the public, Mitterrand presented the image of a distinguished statesman – the devoted husband to Danielle, his First Lady, and a pillar of French political life. But behind those Elysée Palace doors? Let's just say Monsieur le Président was clocking overtime in the double-life department. He had a longtime mistress, Anne, and together they had a daughter named Mazarine. She was kept so hush-hush that she might as well have been in the witness protection program of French high society.

For years, Mazarine lived a clandestine existence, growing up in the shadows of her father's presidency. Imagine being a teenager and having to hide who your dad is – not because he's a secret agent or Batman, but because he's the president juggling two families. It sounds like a plot from *The Crown* meets *Gossip Girl*, with the Eiffel Tower as a backdrop. The French press knew hints of "something" (powerful men with secret mistresses being practically a French tradition and an open secret at that), but they played along with a wink and a nod. Privacy laws in France are stricter than a macaron recipe, and there was an unspoken agreement to let Mitterrand have his *cinq à sept* life (that classic French euphemism for an affair – literally "5 to 7," the time of day lovers meet). And boy, did he take that concept and run with it, living what some joked was a triple life by the end.

The secret officially strolled into the spotlight in 1994, late in Mitterrand's second term, when a bold magazine cover revealed father and daughter together. Suddenly, the whole country was introduced to Mazarine's existence – and in classic French fashion, a collective Gallic shrug ensued among many. "Oh, the president has a hidden daughter? Eh bien, c'est la vie."

But the real dramatic climax came at Mitterrand's funeral in January 1996. In a scene that could have been orchestrated by a Hollywood director, there stood two women side by side by his grave: his widow Danielle and his mistress Anne, united in grief. And right there with them was young Mazarine, mourning a father who had kept her a secret until the very end. The three of them together in public for the first time – a literal family reunion in front of the nation and, awkwardly, at a gravesite. If there were ever a photo to capture the phrase "double life," it was that funeral snapshot of wife and mistress sharing an umbrella, quite possibly exchanging polite yet knowing smiles.

Through wry smiles and raised eyebrows, France digested the news that their late leader had been a family man in the most complicated sense. Internationally, people were agog — imagine if a U.S. President had a secret kid and everyone only found out at his funeral! Cable news would implode. But in France, many took it in stride, as if to say, "We loved him for his culture and politics, not his monogamy." The whole saga, equal parts tragic and darkly comic, serves up a lesson: people are complicated, leaders included. Mitterrand's double life was a reminder that even those at the pinnacle of power have personal lives messier than a dropped croissant. Secrets may be shrugged off for a while — even for decades — but eventually they stroll out of the shadows, perhaps arm-in-arm at a state funeral. And when they do, oh là là, what a dramatic entrance they make.

5.3 The King's DNA Surprise

When you think "royal decree," you probably don't imagine it coming in the form of a DNA test result. But that's exactly how one saga in the Belgian royal family reached its climax. King Albert II of Belgium likely never envisioned that one day he'd be in a situation straight out of a daytime talk show — *"Your Majesty... in the case of Delphine, you are the father!"* — but life had that plot twist in store.

Rewind a few decades: back in the late 1960s, Albert (then a young prince) had an affair with a woman named Baroness Sybille de Selys Longchamps. From this royal fling came a daughter, Delphine, born in

1968. Of course, this being a serious no-no in the royal rulebook, the existence of little Delphine was swept under the plush palace rug. Officially, she was just another Belgian citizen, while Albert went on to become King, smiling and waving next to Queen Paola as if he didn't have a care (or a kid) in the world.

But secrets, especially ones with DNA, have a way of popping up like a persistent jack-in-the-box. As Delphine grew up to be an artist, she also grew more certain – and vocal – about who her father was. Imagine knowing the king is *probably* your dad, but he's acting like you're a stranger. That's some next-level royal drama right there.

For years, Albert II denied her claims harder than a suspect on a crime show. Even as whispers swirled and evidence mounted, he remained as unmoved as one of those somber portraits in the royal gallery. Delphine, however, refused to be a footnote in a king's story. She took her paternity case to court in what became a very public legal battle. The tabloids had a field day – it was like a real-life episode of *The Crown: Brussels Edition*, with every twist and turn scrutinized.

Finally, in 2020, after literally decades of denial (and after Albert abdicated the throne in 2013, perhaps thinking a retired king could more easily dodge the issue), science spoke up. A court-ordered DNA test came back with the royal mic drop of truths: a 99.999% certainty that Albert was Delphine's biological father. Cue the dramatic music and, presumably, some royal sweating.

Under legal and moral pressure – not to mention mounting public side-eye – the former king did something few expected: he acknowledged

Delphine as his daughter. This wasn't just a quiet "okay, fine, she's mine" in a lawyer's office either. Delphine was officially recognized and even granted the title "Princess of Belgium," because if you're going to be acknowledged, you might as well go all the way to princess status, right?

The tale of King Albert and Princess Delphine is a modern mash-up of fairy tale and reality TV. One day you're a commoner fighting to be recognized; the next, you're literally a princess attending family events with the folks who pretended you didn't exist. It's equal parts heartwarming and absurd. Imagine the first awkward royal family gathering – "Pass the peas, please, and oh, hello *half-sister*, delighted to finally meet you after 50 years."

The whole saga teaches a very contemporary lesson: not even kings can hide from DNA. Blue blood is still blood, and science doesn't give a hoot about royal reputation. In an age of 23andMe and viral secrets, the truth will out, even if it has to drag a king out of denial. The irony is rich: a man who wore a crown had to bow to a paternity test. If that isn't poetic justice (or poetic *just DNA*), what is?

5.4 Grandma's Lifetime of Lies

Not all hidden children belong to presidents and kings; sometimes they're tucked away in the attic of our everyday family trees. Case in point: one Reddit user's grandmother – a sweet old lady by all outward accounts – who decided to drop a bombshell on her deathbed that left the whole family reeling. You know those old jokes about the "milkman's baby"? Well, Grandma's story was literally that, minus the joke.

As the tale goes, back in the 1940s, Grandma had a youthful fling with the local milkman (apparently those daily dairy deliveries came with extra cream, nudge nudge). She became pregnant, a huge scandal-in-the-making in that era, and ultimately gave the baby up for adoption in secret. Then she moved on, got married to Grandpa, raised a family, baked her apple pies, knitted those Christmas sweaters – the quintessential grandma life – all while carrying this hidden chapter in her story.

For decades, not a peep about the child she had brought into the world and then relinquished. Imagine the weight of that secret. Grandma went through holidays and reunions listening to quips about the mailman or milkman – the running gags when a kid had the wrong eye color – all while thinking, "If you only knew."

It's almost admirable how steadfastly she kept mum. Perhaps in her mind she thought she was "protecting" her family from scandal, or perhaps protecting herself from judgment.

But as anyone who's watched a soap opera knows, these kinds of secrets have a nasty habit of bursting out eventually, like a long-lost cousin showing up at the doorstep. In Grandma's case, the reveal came at the eleventh hour – literally. On her deathbed, surrounded by loved ones bracing for final words of wisdom, she instead comes out with: "I had a child with the milkman and I've never told anyone." Mic drop. Cue stunned silence, followed by a flurry of "Wait, what did she just say?!"

The family, understandably, was shocked. It was as if a plot twist had been edited into their family history at the last possible moment. There was Grandpa, likely gobsmacked that his dearly departed had harbored this news since Truman was President. Mom and Dad (her children) suddenly had to recalibrate their entire understanding of Grandma's life – not to mention realize they have a half-sibling out there somewhere!

Once the initial shock subsided, the family did what modern families do: they turned to the internet and DNA tests to track down this mystery relative. And lo and behold, they connected with the child (now obviously a grown adult, possibly with their own kids – meaning a whole branch of relatives nobody knew existed). Picture the first meeting: a bunch of folks who've only ever known each other as abstract "DNA matches" or voices on the phone, coming together for a super-awkward, super-heartwarming reunion. It's the kind of story that would lead on the evening news if it weren't so personal – instead it led on Reddit, with thousands of strangers upvoting this real-life family plot twist.

Grandma's lifetime of lies, as harsh as that label sounds, came from a place of the social strictures of her time. It's easy to judge her, but one can also see it through a sympathetic lens: a young woman in the 1940s facing a pregnancy out of wedlock had limited options and a ton of shame foisted upon her. The humorous silver lining (because we have to find one) is how the family handled the revelation.

Sure, there were likely tears and some anger – "Seriously, Grandma?!" – but there was also this bizarre joy in discovery. New relatives! A bigger family tree! It's like one of those TV show episodes where they surprise someone with a relative they didn't know they had; except it's your actual life. In a satirical sense, one could say Grandma played the longest con game of two truths and a lie, and only on her way out did she finally lose.

The lesson here is part cautionary tale, part uplifting: secrets can last a lifetime, but truth connects generations. And sometimes that truth arrives wearing a milkman's uniform, decades late but finally at the doorstep.

5.5 Founding Father's Hidden Offspring

We cap off our parade of parental secrets with a journey back to the early days of the United States – proof that even the vaunted Founding Fathers weren't above a bit of scandalous extracurricular activity. Thomas Jefferson, author of the Declaration of Independence and third President, is often revered as an almost mythical figure, all Enlightenment ideals and gentlemanly conduct. But history, that sly detective, eventually unmasked Jefferson's own family secret: he fathered multiple children with Sally Hemings, an enslaved woman at his Monticello plantation. It's a revelation that adds a dramatic twist (and a hefty dose of irony) to the story of a man who wrote "all men are created equal" while holding Sally – and their children – in bondage.

For much of American history, the Jefferson-Hemings children were the subject of rumors, whispers, and vehement denials by Jefferson's admirers. It was dismissed as slander by those who couldn't reconcile the author of liberty with the notion of him having a second, secret family of color living in servitude. Yet, within the Hemings family and many African American communities, the story was preserved as oral history – a truth passed down like a guarded family recipe. The idea that Jefferson had kids with Sally Hemings was like a ghost that haunted the halls of

Monticello: occasionally visible, often denied, but always there in the shadows.

Fast forward to 1998, when science decided to weigh in on the matter. DNA testing entered the chat like a modern-day Alexander Hamilton dropping truth in a pamphlet. By comparing genetic markers from Jefferson's known descendants and Hemings descendants, the tests effectively shouted from the rooftops: "Yes, Jefferson was their father. Cue the fireworks." Well, perhaps fireworks are too celebratory – it was more like a collective national *gulp*.

The confirmation landed like a plot twist in the national narrative. Imagine the faces at Jeffersonian dinner tables across the country when the news broke – some aghast, some vindicated. It was as if a chapter from a steamy historical novel had been plopped into real-life history books. The Founding Father had a hidden family, and not just any family – a family born into slavery, the very institution he outwardly claimed to abhor yet maintained in practice.

The situation drips with irony so profound that even Alanis Morissette might want to write a song about it (though don't expect it to be a straightforward definition of irony, in keeping with her style). It complicates Jefferson's legacy more than any historiographical debate ever could. Suddenly, depictions of the sage Thomas Jefferson had to make room for Thomas the father of enslaved children – children he never officially recognized in his lifetime.

Yet, within this story is a deeply human element and even a strange sort of resolution. Many of Jefferson's modern-day descendants, both from the line of his white daughter Martha and the lines of Sally Hemings's children, have come together in reunions at Monticello in recent years. Picture that reunion: people of different races, all tracing back to Jefferson, snapping a big family photo on the lawn of the plantation that witnessed those secret nights over two centuries ago. The image itself is powerful – a living rebuke to the idea that history stays neatly in the past. It's as if Jefferson's genetic legacy laughed at the hypocrisy and said, "We're still here!" In a satirical twist, you might say Jefferson's DNA did what his conscience didn't: acknowledge his whole family.

The lesson that echoes from this saga is one for the ages: truth finds a way out, even if it takes two hundred years and the advent of genetic testing. Identities suppressed by power or prejudice can emerge in the most dramatic, head-turning ways. For a man emblematic of American ideals to have this hidden story come to light – it's a reminder that heroes are often as flawed and complicated as the rest of us. In the end, no secret stays buried forever; eventually, the grandest of patriarchs may have to share the pedestal with the very people he tried to keep in the shadows. And if that's not an American family drama worthy of a Broadway musical (or at least an incredibly juicy podcast), I don't know what is.

Chapter 6

Spies, Lies, and Betrayals – Espionage and Wartime Confessions

Picture a spy spilling their guts decades after the deed, like a suspense novel's epilogue written long after the climax. This chapter serves up a sampler of such confessions – equal parts jaw-dropping and chuckle-worthy. We've got unmasked double agents, late-blooming whistleblowers, and even a case of wartime identity theft so bizarre it sounds like fiction. Each tale shows that even the steeliest secret-keeper might eventually crack, often with timing and twists no one sees coming. So settle in for some historical tea-spilling, complete with modern analogies, pop culture nods, and ironic humor that only hindsight can provide.

6.1 The Last of the Cambridge Spies

Meet John Cairncross: the quiet, unassuming academic who turned out to be the elusive fifth member of Britain's infamous Cambridge spy ring. If this were a heist movie, Cairncross would be the guy in the back studying the blueprints while the others hog the spotlight. In a group of flamboyant double agents with codenames and defectors worthy of Hollywood, John was the softly-spoken fellow you'd trust to water your plants while you're on vacation – and that's exactly what made him so effective as a spy.

By day, Cairncross was a respectable civil servant and scholar. Picture a bespectacled intellectual, the type who corrects your French pronunciation and discusses classical music at dinner parties. No one would peg him as a Soviet informant sneaking glances at classified documents. He blended in better than a chameleon on a tartan sofa.

In the 1940s, while Britain was fighting World War II, this mild-mannered chap passed secrets to the Soviets, helping an ally in wartime (at least in his mind) and playing a dangerous game of loyalty flip-flop. The Cambridge spy ring was like the Spice Girls of espionage – everyone knew the big stars, but there was always that elusive "fifth" member people kept forgetting. Cairncross was essentially the Posh Spice of British spies: low-key, often overlooked, but integral to the group's harmony of mischief.

His outing as a spy didn't come with a dramatic unmasking at the office or a high-speed chase across London. No, John Cairncross's spy career ended with a whimper rather than a bang.

In 1964, he quietly confessed to British intelligence officials. How quiet was this confession? Let's just say it was so under-the-radar that not even the nosiest neighbor noticed. Imagine admitting you stole cookies from the cookie jar, but only whispering it to the cookie jar when nobody else is in the kitchen. That's how secret Cairncross's confession was.

British authorities kept his admission hush-hush – partly to avoid scandal, and perhaps because by then he was out of the spy game and posed no immediate threat. They gave him immunity from prosecution in exchange for his cooperation, essentially telling him, "Thanks for the info, now kindly fade into obscurity."

Fade he did. After 1964, Cairncross slipped away into a quiet life, moving abroad and working as a translator and author. For decades, the public was none the wiser that this polite Scotsman had been feeding intelligence to Moscow.

It wasn't until the 1990s – long after the Cold War had thawed and most people had thrown out their James Bond gadgets – that the full story came to light. Historians and former Soviet spies finally spilled the beans publicly: yep, John was the long-suspected "fifth man" of the Cambridge Five. You can imagine the collective British gasp: "That guy? The one who looked like a Latin professor? Blimey!"

The historical irony is rich. Here was a man who dined with colleagues, strolled the corridors of Whitehall, and presumably attended office holiday parties in a tacky sweater, all while betraying state secrets. And he nearly got away with it in plain sight. It's like discovering the quiet neighbor who always waved hello was running an underground speakeasy in his basement – talk about a suburban scandal! In John's case, the polite civil servant was a spy the whole time, proving that sometimes truth hides in the most boring camouflage.

With the truth finally out, John Cairncross holds a permanent, if peculiar, place in history. He was the last of his notorious spy ring to be unmasked, living just long enough to see his name splashed in the papers as a turncoat – though by then he was more amused retiree than international man of mystery. His story teaches us a timeless lesson:

beware the quiet ones with big brains; they might just be plotting a world-class double-cross between cups of Earl Grey tea.

6.2 The Rosenberg Ring Confession

Now zoom across the pond and forward in time for another long-delayed confession – this time from the height of World War II's atomic espionage drama. Meet Morton Sobell, an American electrical engineer who spent the better part of his life insisting he didn't spy for anyone.

He was the friend and college classmate of Julius Rosenberg, and in the early 1950s they were caught up in one of America's most famous spy cases. Back then, Sobell proclaimed his innocence to every judge, journalist, and relative who would listen. For over fifty years, Sobell was like that one uncle who swears he didn't break the vintage lamp in Grandma's living room – and sticks to the lie at every Thanksgiving. He served 18 years in prison for conspiracy to commit espionage (while Julius and Ethel Rosenberg, as everyone remembers, met a far grimmer fate). Upon release, Sobell kept a low profile and mostly stayed out of the spotlight, popping up occasionally to reiterate "I didn't do it" in interviews.

But time has a funny way of loosening lips and easing guilt's grip. Flash forward to 2008. Morton Sobell was 91 years old – an age when most people's biggest secret confession is sneaking an extra candy past the grandkids.

Out of the blue, in this late twilight of his life, Sobell casually changed his tune. In a calm, almost shrugging admission to a New York Times reporter, he acknowledged that, yes, he had indeed passed along military secrets to the Soviet Union during World War II. Oh, and by the way, Julius Rosenberg had been his co-conspirator, just as the prosecutors had claimed all along. In the spy world, this was a mic drop moment – delivered not with bombast but with the tired sigh of a nonagenarian who decided it was finally time to come clean.

The contrast was stark. Here was a man who had denied everything for decades, now confessing with the same level of emotion you'd use to recount a weather report. It was as if he'd spent a lifetime vehemently denying he ate the last slice of cake, only to say at dessert fifty years later, "Actually, I did eat it – pass the coffee, please." The casual tone of Sobell's confession was almost comical. No dramatic courtroom reveal, no tearful apology – just a matter-of-fact acknowledgment, as if the whole thing had been a minor misunderstanding over a misplaced set of car keys.

What prompted this late-in-life burst of honesty? Perhaps age made him reflective; perhaps he didn't want to take the secret to the grave. Or maybe he figured, "What are they going to do, put a 91-year-old back in jail?"

In any case, Sobell's confession in 2008 provided closure to a chapter of Cold War history that had lingered unresolved. It was the final piece of the Rosenberg puzzle clicking into place after half a century. Of course, it also left many people shaking their heads – including the Rosenbergs' surviving family – since his decades of denial had allowed a passionate innocence campaign to flourish. One imagines some of his old supporters felt a bit like the rug was pulled out from under them: "Morton, you mean to tell us now that you did it? After all those marches and petitions? Thanks a lot, pal."

Sobell's story is a poignant (and slightly humorous) reminder that truth has its own timetable. Sometimes it comes out immediately with trumpets blaring, and sometimes it sneaks up like an old man shuffling into a reunion, muttering an overdue confession. In the theater of espionage, Sobell's act was the slow-burn drama with an ending that was both satisfying and a tad absurd. Better late than never, they say – and in Morton Sobell's case, "late" was an understatement.

6.3 Deep Throat Unmasked

Next up on our confession tour: a trip to Washington, D.C., where one of the biggest political mysteries of the 20th century was solved by a simple statement in 2005: "I'm the guy they called Deep Throat." The speaker? W. Mark Felt, a former FBI second-in-command, delivering the mother of all self-reveals. For over thirty years, Deep Throat's identity was the grand parlor game of American politics. Who was the secret informant that helped Washington Post reporters Bob Woodward and Carl Bernstein take down President Nixon in the Watergate scandal? It was the ultimate whodunit – a mystery that spawned books, Hollywood dramatizations, and enough speculation to keep D.C. gossip circles buzzing through many a cocktail party.

Mark Felt had been high on the list of suspected Deep Throats. Still, he denied it repeatedly over the years, even in his own memoirs. He was like a superhero guarding his secret identity – a real-life Clark Kent, if

Superman had decided to leak government secrets in parking garages and then go home to deny everything to Lois Lane.

Felt watched for decades as "Deep Throat" became a cultural icon: depicted in films as a trench-coated shadow with a cigarette, referenced in history classes, even lending his nickname to countless subsequent scandals. Imagine being secretly famous – your alter ego is on the lips of every history buff and journalist, yet you can't stand up and say, "Surprise! It was me." That's some serious anonymous fame.

By 2005, Mark Felt was an elderly gentleman of 91, living a quiet retirement in California. Perhaps the weight of the secret, or a desire for a legacy, finally tipped the scales. With a little nudging from his family (who sensed that a movie deal or two might be in the offing), Felt agreed to go public. It happened in the most modern way possible for such an old-school secret: an article in Vanity Fair magazine. Not a congressional hearing, not a solemn press conference – a glossy magazine scoop complete with stylish prose. How very Hollywood for a G-man who used to skulk in the shadows.

When the world learned that Mark Felt was Deep Throat, the D.C. drama meter went off the charts. News channels ran breathless retrospectives; Woodward and Bernstein finally confirmed it with a mix of relief and nostalgia.

It was as if the masked singer had ripped off the mask on live TV – except in this case the singer was a nonagenarian ex-FBI guy, and the song was the tale of how he helped topple a president. The cultural aftershocks of Watergate got a late aftershock of their own. People who lived through the '70s suddenly felt a rush of memories (and possibly the urge to dig out their old bell-bottoms). Younger folks got a crash course in why every political scandal ends in "-gate." And Hollywood? Oh, Hollywood was delighted – within a couple of years, there was a TV movie about Felt, and whispers of more.

The irony of the leaker seeking recognition after all those years didn't go unnoticed. Deep Throat, the man who stayed hidden out of necessity, now wanted a bit of the limelight for himself (or at least his family wanted it for him). It's a bit like Batman strolling into a press conference well after Gotham is safe and saying, "Yes, it was I who saved the city. Autographs later, please." Either way, Mark Felt's confession gave us one of the most satisfying "big reveals" in modern history. The grand mystery was solved, the credits rolled, and Deep Throat could finally breathe easy – preferably without all that cigarette smoke.

6.4 A Twin's Betrayal in Vietnam

Just when you think wartime secrets couldn't get more bizarre, along comes a tale straight out of a soap opera writer's wildest dreams. This one involves identical twins, the chaos of the Vietnam War, and a lifelong lie that would make even the boldest liars blush. It's the story of a dying veteran who confessed that he had swapped identities with his dead twin brother during the war. If you're already thinking, "Wait, what?" you're not alone.

This confession is the kind of twist that would get rejected in a movie script for being too unbelievable – except it evidently happened.

Let's set the scene: Two twin brothers go off to fight in Vietnam. We'll call them Brother A and Brother B for simplicity. In the fog of war – bullets flying, danger all around – one brother is killed in action. A tragedy, but sadly not an uncommon one.

What happened next, however, was anything but ordinary. The surviving twin, shell-shocked and perhaps not in the soundest frame of mind, decided to swap dog tags and identities with his deceased brother. In other words, he made it look like he had died, and that his fallen brother was the one who survived. Then he went home to assume his dead twin's life, leaving everyone – including their family – believing the wrong son had returned from the war.

It's one part tragic sacrifice, one part identity theft, and one part daytime-soap deceit. This soldier pulled off the ultimate twin switcheroo. Imagine the Thanksgiving dinners he endured, listening to his "own" eulogy year after year as the family spoke fondly of the brother they *thought* had died – who was actually him. It was like attending his own funeral in disguise, year after year, before carving the turkey. Every time an old war buddy or relative would reminisce about the departed twin ("He was such a good kid, shame what happened to him"), the surviving brother had to play along, nodding solemnly about... well, about himself. Talk about awkward.

For decades he kept this jaw-dropping secret, perhaps out of a warped sense of survivor's guilt or the sheer impossibility of coming clean. After all, how do you even begin to tell your own mother that the wrong son came home from the war?

Only as he lay on his deathbed, many years later, did this veteran finally come clean. The secret came tumbling out – a final, cathartic unload of a burden he'd carried his whole life. One imagines the surviving family members' faces looked like they'd seen a ghost, because in a sense, they had. The brother they thought they'd lost in war had been the one at the dinner table all along. Cue the dramatic organ music, because this is the part where a lesser story would cut to commercial break with everyone in stunned silence.

The tragic absurdity of maintaining such a lifelong lie is hard to overstate. It's heart-wrenching that war trauma drove someone to these lengths. At the same time, the sheer scope of the deception leaves you marveling at how he pulled it off. He essentially lived his brother's life as his own — a bureaucratic and emotional nightmare of epic proportions. We're talking about forging a whole identity and carrying that secret through every moment, big and small. The emotional toll must have been immense.

In a way, this twin-swapping saga is a dark mirror of the playful pranks twins often pull. Trading places for a day in school is one thing; trading lives after a battlefield tragedy is on a whole other level. It forces us to think about identity and how war can shatter and reshape it. Also, it's a stark reminder that truth really can be stranger (and more twisted) than fiction. If you ever complained about a sibling borrowing your clothes without asking, just be glad they didn't borrow your entire identity.

6.5 The KGB's Man in the Vatican – (Redacted)

Now for our final tale... oh, wait. It seems this section has been REDACTED in the interest of international security and possibly to avoid a very awkward phone call from Vatican City. (I wish I were kidding.) You see, dear reader, the story that was supposed to go here was so juicy, so classified, that higher powers (and we do mean *higher* powers) intervened. Apparently, when you mix Cold War espionage with the Holy See, you get a story hotter than a habanero – and it sets off all the alarm bells in legal departments from here to Rome.

What can we say about "The KGB's Man in the Vatican" without getting excommunicated or worse? Well, we can confirm that it involved a Soviet spy sneaking around the Vatican's hallowed halls in an era when incense and intrigue were both thick in the air. Picture a clever agent – let's call him Comrade X – disguised as a humble priest or maybe a lowly librarian in the Vatican Archives, but with a direct line to Moscow. Imagine him slipping secret documents under the nose of cardinals and curators, hiding microfilm in communion wafers (okay, probably not that, the logistics are tricky), and conducting clandestine midnight meetings in candlelit chapels. It's the kind of tale that would make Dan Brown rub his hands together with glee. In fact, throw in a dash of Tom Hanks in a tweed jacket, and you've practically got the next blockbuster sequel to *The Da Vinci Code*.

Of course, all of the above is hypothetical, because the *real* details are, alas, censored. Did Comrade X influence papal decisions? Was there a dramatic confession in the Sistine Chapel as Michelangelo's saints looked on in shocked silence? Were Swiss Guards chasing a KGB operative through Saint Peter's Basilica, cassock hems flying and secret ciphers spilling from hidden pockets? We're not saying it happened, but we're not *not* saying it happened. (The author winks conspiratorially here, but that's hard to convey in print.)

In the spirit of full disclosure – or rather, cheeky non-disclosure – let's just embrace the redaction. Think of this section as the classified file you *can't* access, the missing episode of your favorite spy series that was too controversial to air. The very fact that it's redacted should tell you how epic it *might* have been. The void sparks your imagination: perhaps it's teeming with scandalous revelations about espionage in the halls of the Vatican, or maybe it's just a bunch of recipes for borscht hidden in Latin prayer books. We'll never know!

And so, we end this chapter on a playful note of censorship. Consider it a reminder that some secrets remain so secret, even a tell-all book has to zip its lips. But don't worry – if anyone asks, you didn't hear it from me.

Chapter 7

Who Are You Really? – Fake Identities and Double Lives

You think you know someone, and then—plot twist—they're not at all who they claimed to be. In this chapter, we dive into real stories of people who led extraordinary double lives, each more unbelievable than the last. It's a wild ride through jazz clubs and jungles, suburban living rooms and secret bank heists, all told with an irreverent wink. Along the way we'll sprinkle in some modern analogies and maybe even a heartfelt lesson or two (buried under layers of satire, of course). Buckle up: truth really is stranger than fiction, and sometimes funnier too.

7.1 The Jazz Legend Who Wasn't

Billy Tipton lounges at home in the 1950s with his dog and a newspaper, looking every bit the ordinary family man. But on stage, Tipton was a dapper jazz pianist and bandleader – and he had a secret that would make even the most method of actors spit out their drink. For decades, Billy lived as a man, touring the mid-century jazz circuit, marrying several women (five called themselves *Mrs. Tipton* over the years), and adopting three sons. His friends, fellow musicians, and even his wives had no clue that Billy had been assigned female at birth – not until 1989 when, in a dramatic final act, his own body revealed the truth. Tipton collapsed from a health issue and paramedics made the shocking discovery as they tried to save him: the suave old jazzman was biologically female. Cue the scandalized headlines screaming "HE WAS A SHE!" – the ultimate spoiler alert delivered by the Grim Reaper.

It's hard to overstate the dedication this required. Billy Tipton essentially gave an Oscar-worthy performance for fifty *years* without so much as a coffee break. By day, he was tickling the ivories in smoky clubs, binding his chest and dressing in natty suits like a 1940s Cary Grant. By night, he was... well, still in character, even in the privacy of home. His wives reportedly never knew his secret; he told them war injuries had rendered him unable to have biological children, hence the adoptions. Talk about commitment to a role! Daniel Day-Lewis method-acting for a few months has nothing on Billy living 24/7 in costume. At one point, Tipton even turned down a record deal and a big tour, possibly to keep his life low-key and avoid physical exams – passing up fame to protect his truth. In an age when societal rules said "women can't be jazz bandleaders," Billy Tipton said "hold my saxophone" and rewrote his script.

The nature of performance and "passing" takes center stage in Tipton's story. We *all* perform to some degree – putting on a customer-service voice, curating our Instagram lives – but Billy's performance was literal and lifelong. He navigated the world with the deftness of an actor who never breaks character. It's the kind of story that makes you question identity itself: Is it defined by the body, or the role one plays? Billy clearly chose the latter, right up until the body's ultimate betrayal at the end, when the final curtain was pulled back. In a way, it's the most dramatic jazz solo ever improvised: one that ended on a revelatory note he never meant the audience to hear.

This tale resonates today in our culture of reinvention and celebrity mystique. Think of secretive stars like famously private pop icon Sia hiding behind wigs, or actors like Tobey Maguire who managed to keep a low profile for years – only Tipton took it to an extreme. It's as if Hannah Montana lived her whole life as two people and never did the big onstage "Best of Both Worlds" reveal. We're obsessed with reinvention: from Madonna's constant metamorphoses to Lady Gaga's male alter ego on the VMAs, we eat up stories of people becoming someone new. Yet Billy's transformation wasn't a publicity stunt or a weekend role-play; it was life or death in an era that wouldn't have accepted him otherwise. The lesson (wrapped in satire): Life can be a performance, but unlike a movie, you don't always get to choose when the credits roll or what surprises appear in the post-credits scene. Tipton's saga reminds us that authenticity can wear a disguise – and that sometimes the most genuine life is lived in the costume that fits your soul, if not your body.

7.2 The Ultimate Imposter Brother

If you thought fake identities in music were dramatic, wait till you hear about the Vietnam War twin swap – it's a doozy. Picture a gritty war movie meets a soap opera evil-twin episode: Two identical twin brothers go off to war in the late 1960s. They're so alike even their fellow soldiers can't tell them apart. Now imagine one twin doesn't survive... except he does, because it's actually the other twin who returns home, assuming his dead brother's identity. Yes, really.

According to a chilling deathbed confession years later, one twin murdered his brother in Vietnam, stole his dog tags, and slipped back into civilian life as the brother. He fooled *everyone*, even the deceased brother's wife, into thinking he was the one who died and that the twin who lived was gone. (Take a moment to untangle that — it's Twin Shenanigans 101, only with way higher stakes.) How on earth did nobody notice? The confession revealed a dark irony: the war had changed him so much — hardened his features, weighed on his soul — that when he came home "he was so unrecognizable from the man he was before, no one could tell". In other words, trauma became the ultimate disguise.

This is identity theft on a Shakespearean level, with a dash of *Days of Our Lives*. Evil twins are a trope as old as daytime TV, but usually the victim isn't an actual identical twin brother! Here, it was fraternal betrayal beyond Cain and Abel. One can only imagine Thanksgiving dinners in that household. Well, actually, you can't — because *no one knew*. The surviving twin carried on the charade for decades, living his brother's life, likely celebrating birthdays and anniversaries that weren't his, maybe even looking into the eyes of "his" children knowing they weren't biologically his. The psychological gymnastics required are mind-blowing. It's the kind of secret that would send Freud running from the therapy couch. Picture this guy in group therapy: "Hi, I'm... uh... *Bob*. I have imposter syndrome, *literally*. Also I killed my twin." That's a showstopper at Trauma Anonymous.

Of course, such a colossal lie cannot stay buried forever. On his deathbed, wracked by guilt and facing the Big Judgment (or maybe just tired of keeping track of who he was supposed to be), the twin finally confessed to a nurse what he had done. I like to imagine the nurse's face went through several cartoonish iterations of shock. The family, upon learning the truth, must have felt like the ground shifted beneath them. The man they'd loved for a lifetime was, in fact, someone else entirely. It's a twist ending worthy of an M. Night Shyamalan film – *"The Brother"*.

Satirically speaking, this story has everything: murder, identity theft, a twin trope, and a final-act confession. It's almost too perfect for Hollywood, yet too insane *to* be Hollywood (no one would buy the script!). It also highlights a strange aspect of human nature: the lengths one might go to escape or erase who they are. Maybe the surviving twin couldn't face going home as himself – maybe guilt made him believe his brother deserved to "live" more than he did. So he quite literally became him. It's both an act of extreme selfishness (he *did* kill his brother, after all – minor detail) and extreme dedication to a lie.

And what about that poor wife who unknowingly spent her life with the wrong twin? This is like the darkest version of "The Parent Trap" imaginable – *The Sibling Trap*, if you will, with a body count. The family dynamics are horrifyingly fascinating. Did the twin ever slip up and call himself by his original name? Did he avoid old friends who might notice subtle differences ("Gee, you're acting like your brother used to")? The story is tragic, yes, but also perversely rich for satire because it underscores just how absurd real life can be. The guilt that finally forced the truth out is the grim punchline: you can steal someone else's identity, but you can't fully escape your own conscience. In the end, the truth parachuted in, late but undeniable. The takeaway? If you think your family has issues, just be glad your last Zoom call didn't involve someone admitting they're secretly your uncle Gary wearing an Uncle Larry mask. Some double lives are *really* not worth the two-for-one deal.

7.3 The Ballad of Mr. and Mrs. Wilson

Let's take a breather from homicide and talk about good old domestic duplicity. Remember Mr. Wilson from Chapter 4.1? (If you need a refresher: he's the fellow who managed to accumulate four wives living separate lives, like a door-to-door salesman selling bigamy instead of vacuum cleaners.) Yes, *that* Mr. Wilson – the original overachiever in the matrimony department. We chronicled his quadruple life already, with jaws on the floor. At one point we joked about inventing a hypothetical fifth wife just to see if he could handle a basketball team's worth of spouses, but honestly the truth was so far-fetched we decided fiction could take the day off. Reality outpaced fiction with Mr. Wilson; any more wives and we'd have to assume he had a time-turner or a clone. Four was plenty, thank you.

The absurdity of a man juggling four separate marriages is both mind-boggling and darkly comedic. Alexander "Alec" Wilson (as it turned out, this was based on a real historical figure) was a *serial bigamist* who maintained multiple families who knew nothing of each other. It sounds like a Netflix drama, except if you wrote it into a script people might say "Nah, too unrealistic." His real-life wives only discovered the truth after his death, leading to the most awkward crossover episode of all time (imagine four grieving "widows" meeting at the funeral – it's empathy meets farce). Mr. Wilson managed a quadruple life through elaborate lies, a ridiculous amount of organization, and probably a Rolodex the size of an encyclopedia to keep all those birthdays and anniversaries straight. If he were around today, he'd need four separate smartphones and an army of virtual assistants to juggle that many Google Calendars.

Modern double lives, however, have evolved with technology (and thankfully with far less legal marriage fraud... usually). In today's irreverent spin on the Mr. Wilson scenario, we have tech bros with burner phones for their side communications, and suburban dads with secret podcast empires that their family has no clue about. It's true – you could be mowing the lawn next to someone who has an alter ego as a famous anonymous political podcaster or the lead singer of a Viking metal band on Spotify. At least Mr. Wilson's misadventures were analog; now the internet allows anyone to cultivate a second life from the comfort of their basement. Is that better or worse? Hard to say, but it's comedy gold. "Honey, I'm going to the store for milk," he says, when actually he's sneaking off to record his weekly True Crime ASMR podcast under a pseudonym.

And let's not forget the polyamory TikTok influencers, the 21st-century twist on multiple marriages. Unlike Mr. Wilson, these folks *broadcast* their many relationships – but often to an audience of strangers online, while keeping things hush-hush in the PTA carpool. It's as if the ethos is: one life for the algorithm, another for the neighbors. Mr. Wilson could only dream of the kind of compartmentalization today's double-life-livers achieve. One minute they're posting choreographed dances with two partners in matching outfits, the next they're at the office water cooler nodding along as a coworker raves about monogamy.

The running joke here is that truth really *is* stranger than fiction. We toyed with adding a fictitious fifth wife to Mr. Wilson's tale, but why bother when some Silicon Valley coder might be quietly running five dating app profiles under different names right now? The comedic (and slightly unsettling) reality is that living a double life has never been easier – or more absurd. You can practically have an alternate identity for each social media platform. Your LinkedIn self, your Reddit troll self, your family-man Facebook self, and your secret OnlyFans self could all be different "yous," and who's to know? At least until, like Mr. Wilson, it all comes crashing down when worlds inevitably collide (they always do).

So, what's the heartfelt takeaway amid this snark? Probably that maintaining one honest life is hard enough – maintaining multiples is a circus act destined to go hilariously awry. Mr. Wilson's legacy (apart from seven children and four very justifiably upset widows) is a reminder that eventually someone's going to trip over the truth. And no matter how many burner phones you have, there's only one of *you* to go around. As any sitcom bigamist or TikTok poly throuple might admit: the truth tends to leak, and when it does, you'd better have an excellent explanation… or a really good lawyer.

7.4 The Man Who Fell to Earth (Twice)

Strap in for this one: the tale of Ted Conrad, the gentleman bank robber who literally *became* someone else and almost got away with it. It's 1969 in Cleveland, Ohio, and 20-year-old Conrad works as a bank teller. He's an unassuming, all-American kid by all accounts – except he has a grand plan brewing in that head of his. See, Ted had watched Steve McQueen in *The Thomas Crown Affair* one too many times and became *obsessed* with the idea of the suave bank heist. So what does he do? On a Friday afternoon, he engineers a moment alone with the vault (perhaps telling a coworker to take off early, TGIF and all that). He then stuffs $215,000 in cash (worth over $1.7 million today) into a paper bag, walks out of the bank, and vanishes into thin air. Talk about a Friday feeling! The bank doesn't even realize the money's missing until the following Monday, giving our man a nice head start. It was one of the biggest Cleveland heists ever, and Ted Conrad pulled it off without even drawing a gun – just pure chutzpah and impeccable timing.

Now comes the second act: the *reinvention*. Ted Conrad said goodbye to his old identity like it was an out-of-season wardrobe. He fled to the East Coast, eventually landing in the Boston area, and assumed the alias "Thomas Randele." New name, new birthday (he even adjusted his birth year to appear two years older, for extra believability), new life. And here's the kicker: *Tom Randele lived an utterly ordinary, even boringly wholesome life.* He got married in the early 1980s, had a daughter, became a golf pro at a country club, then a luxury car salesman. He paid his taxes, hosted backyard barbecues, made friends – one of whom was an FBI agent, believe it or not. The audacity and irony are almost too perfect: for 52 years, the authorities hunted high and low for Ted Conrad, not realizing he was playing the role of genial Mr. Randele, the friendly neighbor who might help jump-start your car or give you golf tips, living just a few towns over from them. Talk about hiding in plain sight!

To maintain a lie for over half a century is an act of bureaucratic acrobatics as much as psychological ones. Just think of the paperwork involved. Conrad had to forge or finagle a Social Security number, driver's license, and all the trappings of legal existence under a fake name. Ever filled out a passport application? Now imagine doing that as someone who doesn't technically exist. One slip-up and he'd be toast. But "Tom Randele" was meticulous. He even filed for bankruptcy in 2014 as Tom, signing documents that decades later would help investigators finally confirm he was really Ted. (In a comedic twist, it was that paper trail – the very thing he had to create to live normally – that led to his unmasking. Let it be noted: even in a life of crime, you can't escape *paperwork* forever.)

For 52 years, Ted/Tom effectively performed a one-man show: "The Normal Life of an Upstanding Citizen." And by all accounts, it was a smash hit. He never got arrested for anything else, never aroused suspicion. U.S. Marshals chased leads across the country for decades, while Tom sipped lemonade in his yard and paid his HOA dues on time. It's the Everyman Criminal archetype – the idea that the guy next door could secretly be an outlaw – brought to life. If this were fiction, we'd expect him to be looking over his shoulder dramatically every time he heard sirens. But apparently, he was cool as a cucumber. *This* is midwestern grit meets New England respectability in one man. Perhaps the biggest challenge of his life as Tom wasn't dodging the law, but keeping a straight face when friends excitedly discussed that episode of Unsolved Mysteries about the missing Cleveland bank thief (oh, the irony – yes, his case was on TV). One imagines him gripping his iced tea a little tighter during those conversations.

In the end, reality caught up, as it always does. Suffering from terminal illness in 2021, Tom finally confessed to his wife and daughter that he'd been living under a fake identity – that he was Ted Conrad, the long-sought fugitive. Can you imagine that family meeting? "Ladies, I have something to tell you…" It's the kind of revelation that usually involves the phrase "secret family" or "hidden fortune," but in this case it was "I *am* the hidden fortune, sort of." His daughter later said he dropped the bomb while they were literally watching a crime show on TV (because life has a sense of humor). A few months after his confession, Ted/Tom passed away, and shortly thereafter law enforcement finally put the puzzle pieces together and publicly identified him as the long-lost thief. The mystery that lasted a lifetime was solved – just a tad too late to slap cuffs on him. As one U.S. Marshal put it, Conrad's disappearance lasted 52 years, "a few months longer than he did".

What do we make of this epic double life? For one, it highlights the myth of the "new start." We always hear you can't truly run from your problems, but Ted Conrad came *remarkably* close. He lived out essentially an entire second life, proof that with enough daring and a bit of luck, you *can* outrun consequences… for a while. It took illness and old age to slow him down. From a satirical angle, there's almost a charming audacity to how ordinary he became. No continued life of crime, no dramatic heel turn – he robbed one bank, then decided that was enough excitement and settled into PTA meetings and 9-to-5 normalcy. It's as if D.B. Cooper landed, then immediately started a book club and never looked back.

Yet, even after "falling to Earth" and living quietly, Conrad couldn't fully escape *Ted*. In the final accounting, he chose to reveal the truth to those closest to him. Perhaps he didn't want them to live a lie after he was gone. Or maybe he just *had* to finally shed the character and die as himself. It's oddly poignant: the performance ended on his own terms. The gall it took to do what he did is matched only by the relief that must have come with laying down that burden at the very end. The lesson in this lunacy? You might get away with your double life for years, even decades, but eventually you'll either slip up or fess up. Also, if you're considering stealing a fortune, know that you'll still have to pay taxes and possibly even declare bankruptcy like the rest of us schmoes – the universe has a way of equalizing things.

7.5 The SEAL Who Wasn't

Our final tale of double-life derring-do (or more like derring-*don't*) involves something uniquely American: stolen valor – claiming military honors you haven't earned. Consider this scenario: A man spends decades spinning elaborate war stories, telling everyone who'll listen that he was a badass Navy SEAL back in the day. He's got the swagger, the anchor tattoos, the barstool bravery. His family, friends, the guys at the church or VFW hall all believe him. He basks in the respect and deference – after all, Navy SEALs are the stuff of legend. There's only one catch: he never served a single day as a SEAL. The whole persona is as fictional as Rambo.

This is not a hypothetical; versions of this have happened multiple times. One case involved a church deacon in California who for 50 years let everyone believe he was a retired SEAL, fooling even his wife of 41 years and his own children. (That's right: he told *Sunday school* kids about his covert ops, without so much as a wink.) In another, a pastor in Pennsylvania wove such a convincing yarn about Vietnam combat that a local paper wrote a profile on him… only for it to come out that he'd cribbed most of his "memories" from action movies like *Under Siege* and *G.I. Jane*. Yes, he literally lifted scenes involving being waterboarded and kitchen duty from Steven Seagal and Demi Moore, passing them off as his own life events. Give that man a Razzie Award for Worst Original Screenplay – the truth blew up in his face when real SEAL veterans recognized Hollywood when they heard it.

What drives someone to fabricate a hero's life? Satirically, it's almost understandable: who wouldn't want to claim they can kill a man with a paperclip and survived on bugs in the jungle, without actually enduring the misery of BUD/S training? It's the ultimate cheat code to masculinity and respect. These imposters want the heroism without the boot camp, the medals without the battle scars. It's like wanting a Purple Heart as a participation trophy. For years, many of them get away with it, dining out (sometimes literally) on lies. They'll swag around in surplus store camo, maybe flash a bogus military ID for a discount, relishing the wide-eyed "Thank you for your service" accolades. On Facebook they might share patriotic memes and war stories with the gravitas of a seasoned warrior. Their kids grow up thinking dad is basically John Wayne meets Captain America.

But eventually, inevitably, the truth comes calling. In the case of our church deacon, he was exposed by investigative reporters and forced to make a very public apology – I imagine that church potluck got awkward real fast. In other instances, these guys only come clean at the very end of their lives. Deathbed confessions seem to be a running theme in this chapter, and the fake SEAL is no exception. With mortality staring them down, even the most stubborn pretender can feel the weight of years of deceit. One such man finally admitted to his family, as he lay dying, that all his tales of secret missions and valor were lies. The news hit like a torpedo to the hull: imagine realizing the patriarch of your family is not the war hero you believed, but just a regular Joe with an overactive imagination and a moral compass gone awry.

The phenomenon of phony SEALs (and Green Berets, and Marines… equal opportunity liars) became so rampant that actual veterans set up watchdog groups. Former Navy SEAL Don Shipley famously took it upon himself to expose hundreds of imposters, turning it into a one-man crusade (and something of a YouTube series). After the real Navy SEALs killed Osama bin Laden in 2011, these wannabes "came out of the woodwork" trying to soak up second-hand glory. There's comedy in how commonplace it became. It got to where if you met a guy at a bar claiming to be SEAL Team Six, odds were higher that he was Six-Pack Sam from accounting. The culture even gave us the term "stolen valor" – the idea that claiming unearned honor is a kind of theft, an offense to those who truly served. Congress at one point passed the Stolen Valor Act to punish fakers who profit off false claims, because apparently we needed a law to tell grown men not to LARP as war heroes for free stuff.

Now, mid-century masculinity tropes definitely play a part here. In Grandpa's day, a man proved himself through military service (or at least that was the expectation). Those who didn't serve might have felt "less than," and some compensated by inventing tales taller than a Marine's high-and-tight. The difference is Grandpa's white lies about "fighting off a bear in Korea" usually weren't broadcast on social media to thousands. Today's pretenders sometimes build whole online personas around their faux service – until they slip up by, say, wearing the wrong insignia or claiming a rank that defies the space-time continuum (we've seen guys claim to be like 25-year-old Vietnam vets – do the math, buddy). They get outed, and cue the Internet mob with pitchforks and hilarious memes.

So what's the denouement for our ersatz SEAL? In the case of the deathbed confessor, he likely exited this world with a mixture of relief and regret. Relief that he finally told the truth; regret that the truth wasn't as impressive as the lie. His family, left to grapple with the shattered image, might feel anger, or strangely, compassion – realizing that this man felt so inadequate as himself that he spent a lifetime play-acting a part.

Amid the satire here lies that pitiful nugget: a lot of double lives are rooted in yearning. Yearning to be seen, to be admired, to be someone "greater." It's human, if not honorable.

The comedic silver lining? At least these fakers give us some wild stories to tell. And unlike actual special ops missions, we can discuss them openly and laugh. The heartfelt lesson wrapped in this absurdity is one that applies to this whole chapter: be yourself – everyone else is taken, and keeping up a lie is exhausting. Besides, if you lie about yourself, you're basically writing checks your *reputation* can't cash, and one day the truth will collect. Our lineup of Tipton, the twin, Mr. Wilson, Conrad, and the fake SEAL all learned (some the hard way) that double lives have a way of doubling back on you. The truth might be uncomfortable, embarrassing, even dangerous – but when it finally bursts out, it tends to wash away the facade like a pressure hose on a muddy driveway.

So as we close this irreverent chapter of secret identities and double lives, take a moment to appreciate the simple, boring authenticity of your own life. Sure, you might not be a jazz legend or a master spy or a millionaire fugitive – but hey, you also won't have to orchestrate an eleventh-hour confession to clear your conscience. And if you *are* secretly living a double life as you read this, consider this your sign to retire the act while you can. Because as we've seen, the truth makes for the most ridiculous, compelling stories – and it always, always comes out in the end.

Chapter 8

Crimes of Conscience – Guilt, Regret, and Final Justice

8.1 Burning Cross to Broken Heart: Henry Alexander's Late Redemption

In the late 1950s, Henry Alexander was the kind of man who lit up the night for all the wrong reasons – a cross-burning Ku Klux Klansman with a chip on his shoulder and hate in his heart. By day, he was a *respectable* local businessman (even running a plumbing company on Wetumpka Road) and family man; by night, a self-appointed guardian of segregationist "values." It's a tale as American as apple pie – if the pie were laced with arsenic. For years, Henry strutted around Montgomery, Alabama, with the swagger of a bigoted peacock, convinced of his own untouchability. He had escaped justice before – even dodging charges for a 1964 church bombing – so he likely assumed his dark secrets would march him to the grave untouched. Little did he know that *conscience* sometimes has a way of crashing even the liveliest hate parade.

In January 1957, Henry and a trio of Klan buddies decided to "teach a lesson" to Willie Edwards Jr., a 24-year-old Black truck driver who was just minding his own business. Henry, craving importance, had cooked up a lie that Willie made a pass at a white woman – classic racist fiction straight out of the old Southern playbook. The gang kidnapped Willie at gunpoint and drove him to a high bridge over the Alabama River. There, playing judge, jury, and would-be executioner, they gave the terrified man a cruel choice: jump or be shot. Willie jumped to his death, and Henry Alexander's vile boast became deadly reality. For twenty years, the crime went unpunished. When the law finally caught up in the late 1970s, lack of proof of exactly *how* Willie died led a judge to drop the case, and Henry walked free. He returned to his ordinary life – the bigoted businessman who had gotten away with murder, hiding in plain sight behind Sunday church pews and polite smiles.

Fast-forward to the mid-1970s: Henry Alexander, now in his 60s, was facing an enemy he couldn't intimidate – terminal cancer. Turns out, staring death in the face has a way of melting even a hardened heart. On his deathbed in 1976, wracked by guilt (or perhaps just fear of hellfire hotter than any cross he ever burned), Henry finally confessed to his wife what he had done. In a shaky voice, he admitted he had been the ringleader that night on the bridge. "That man never hurt anybody. I caused it," he murmured, regret staining every word. The bluster was gone; in its place was a feeble old man seeking absolution at the 11th hour. His wife – who never even suspected his involvement despite his track record – listened in disbelief. Decades of marriage, and she had *no idea* that the soft-spoken retiree beside her had once been a marauder of the night. (Apparently even a 1960s arrest for bombing a church hadn't clued her in – love *is* blind, and sometimes willfully ignorant.) Henry's confession spilled out: the kidnapping, the forced jump, the long years of living with the secret. He confessed that his entire excuse for targeting Willie was a lie born of his own pathetic need to "feel important" among the Klan. In that fragile moment, the racist lion of Montgomery became a remorseful lamb.

Of course, cynics might say Henry's change of heart was *convenient*. After all, clearing your conscience is a lot easier when you know you won't have to face a jury afterward – the Grim Reaper makes a pretty good retirement plan for avoiding prison. It's the ultimate late-in-life virtue signal: decades of silence, then a grand *mea culpa* when the only person who can punish you is Saint Peter at the pearly gates. American culture has seen this kind of last-minute image rehab before. Think of former segregationist politicians who, once the tides turned, suddenly found God and Gospel choir photo-ops. (George Wallace famously swapped his segregationist battle cries for apologies in a wheelchair, courting Black voters' forgiveness late in life – an act equal parts genuine repentance and reputation makeover.) Henry's deathbed atonement was cut from the same cloth. It's as if he wanted to script a redemptive final scene for himself: the bigot-turned-penitent, hoping history would footnote his cruelty with a mention of remorse. In a darkly satirical way, one could liken it to Darth Vader tossing the Emperor to save Luke – decades of evil, one act of redemption right before the credits roll. Or maybe Henry was more like a scandal-plagued celebrity releasing a tearful apology video from hospice, aiming to cleanse a lifetime of sins with a single performance. Late repentance, meet late-night infomercial.

Yet for all the justifiable cynicism, there is something tragically human in Henry Alexander's final confession. It didn't bring Willie Edwards Jr. back, nor did it bring earthly justice – but it did lay bare the truth, shattering the lie that had cloaked Willie's murder. Henry couldn't change the past, but in his last moments he could at least *own* it. And perhaps that's the cautionary tale here: the ghosts of our misdeeds have a nasty habit of showing up when we're least able to run from them. Henry lived with the ghost of Willie Edwards haunting his conscience for decades. In the end, that ghost won. Henry Alexander died a broken man with a burden finally spoken, leaving the rest of us to grapple with the mess he made.

Moral: Hate may scorch the world in life, but guilt will burn a hole in *you* eventually. It's never too late to renounce your demons – but waiting until your deathbed to find a conscience is the ultimate cop-out. In short, if you plan to become a better person, do it sooner than the last five minutes of the series finale.

8.2 Vigilante Grandpa's Dark Secret: Family Myths on Trial

Everyone has that sweet elderly relative who seems as harmless as a fly. Maybe it's the great-uncle who sneaks you candy at reunions and falls asleep in front of the TV during *Jeopardy!* – a portrait of innocence in orthopedic shoes. Our story here begins with just such a gentle great-uncle, a man who lived his 80-odd years as the very model of geniality. He patted kids on the head, told corny knock-knock jokes, and remained unfailingly polite. Family lore painted him as a saint who could do no wrong. But as it turns out, even the kindest eyes can hide the darkest secrets. On his deathbed, this loveable "Grandpa" figure dropped a bombshell worthy of a prestige true-crime drama: he confessed that, many decades ago, he **killed** his first wife. *Cue the record scratch and collective gasp.* The family myth of pure-hearted Grandpa went up in flames like an overcooked Sunday roast.

As the stunned family members gathered around, our great-uncle – let's call him Seamus for this tale – revealed a chapter of his life that had been buried deeper than an HBO plot twist. Back in the 1950s, in a rural village in Ireland, Seamus's first marriage was nothing like the happy pictures in the old black-and-white photo album. His wife (now *very* late wife) had a vicious streak. According to his deathbed account, Seamus one day discovered her brutally abusing a child – a little one in their extended family – an act of cruelty that sent this ordinarily gentle man into a red mist of rage. In a moment of protective fury and vigilante justice, he did the unthinkable: he ended her life. The details remained scant (a terse Irishman even in his final confession, he spared the family graphic specifics), but he made it clear that the death was no accident. One could imagine a dramatic confrontation by a peat fire on a stormy night, but however it happened, the result was a dead wife and a secret that Seamus carried for the rest of his days.

How did he get away with it? Here the story blurs into conjecture and half-remembered family lore. Perhaps he staged an accident – a tragic tumble off a cliff along the wild Irish coast, or a "drowning" in the bog that no one questioned. Maybe he had help covering it up in that old-village way, whispers among locals ensuring the constabulary never looked too hard. What we do know is that shortly afterward, Seamus emigrated to America, leaving Ireland – and his dark deed – behind him.

To the American relatives, he was just the widower who lost his young bride to misfortune. He eventually remarried, built a new life, and the Irish first wife became a ghost story nobody in the family ever heard. Until that deathbed confession, of course, when the ghost finally spoke. It was the ultimate family secret, unearthed in a hospital room under the fluorescent lights, with a group of bewildered offspring and nieces and nephews saying, *"Wait... what?"* If Netflix's true-crime unit had been there, they'd have had a field day – *Vigilante Grandpa: The Confession* would be trending #1 by next week.

This startling revelation punched a gaping hole in the "myth of family purity." We like to believe our forebears were paragons of virtue or at least amusing eccentrics – not potential cast members of *Criminal Minds*. Yet here was proof that even the sweetest patriarch could harbor a chapter straight out of a Scorsese film. Moral complexity doesn't even begin to cover it. On one hand, Seamus's act was heinous – murder is murder, after all. On the other hand, if his story is true, he saved a child from horrific abuse in the only way he saw fit at the time. Hero or villain? The family was left reeling in that gray zone, trying to reconcile the kindly old man who taught them how to fish with the avenger who once took the law (and a life) into his own hands. It's the kind of ethical pretzel that would make a philosophy professor cackle and a true-crime podcaster drool. A scenario *worthy* of a Netflix prestige series indeed: think *The Crown* meets *Dexter*, with a brogue and a flat cap.

As the shock settled in, some relatives tried to rationalize. "Well, those were different times," an elderly cousin murmured, as if era alone could explain away a secret homicide. Others remembered odd quirks of Seamus's behavior – the way he'd sometimes stare at old family photos in melancholy silence, or how he never tolerated anyone raising a hand to a child in his presence. Red flags that seemed, in hindsight, as obvious as the *Murder, She Wrote* reruns he loved. Of course, in life, hindsight is a luxury. The family's picture of Seamus had been a carefully curated collage that omitted the ugly piece. This is how family legends are built: selective memory glosses over the unsavory bits to maintain the image of a wholesome lineage. We prefer our grandparents as war heroes or hardworking immigrants – not as vigilantes with a body count.

Yet reality is messy. Good people can do terrible things, and bad people can have moments of grace. The deathbed scene had all the drama of a Hollywood finale: a tearful confession, gasps, and one final breath as Seamus exited stage left, leaving everyone to grapple with the truth. One almost expects a streaming service to option the rights. Picture the trailer voiceover: *"He was a kind old soul… with a deadly secret. This fall, family bonds will be tested when truth and legend collide."* In the aftermath, the family did what families do – they argued, they theorized, they reeled. Some forgave the old man posthumously, reasoning that he had acted to protect the innocent. Others were horrified, feeling they'd been living in a lie their whole lives. Thanksgiving dinners would never be the same, that's for sure.

Amid the turmoil, dark humor found its way into the mix. "Guess great-uncle Seamus put the *'die'* in *'diehard family man'*, huh?" quipped one nephew, nervously. Someone joked about checking the backyard of the old homestead for buried secrets, prompting half-serious nods. It's human nature – sometimes you laugh because the alternative is to cry. And as the family confronted this dismantling of their "pure" family narrative, they also bonded over the sheer outrageousness of it. Who knew Grandpa had a plot twist up his sleeve all these years? It made every other family's skeletons – the bankruptcies, the secret adoptions, the quiet alcoholism – seem positively tame. Harmless old folks harboring wild secrets? Check. Suddenly every sweet grandparent in the lineage got a second glance. ("Nana, you sure you never knocked off a drifter in your youth? Just checking!") It's sobering to realize you might not know everything about those closest to you until it's dramatically revealed at the final hour.

Moral: Families, like Netflix thrillers, are full of surprise twists. The lovable old relative might just have a chapter out of a crime novel. So love your kin, but don't put anyone on a pedestal – the view from up there can hide some pretty dark shadows. In other words, even the nicest grandpa might have been a *bad hombre* when provoked, so keep an open mind (and maybe a good lawyer on speed dial, just in case).

8.3 The Freezer Mom's Last Apology: Ice-Cold Secrets in Suburbia

On the surface, the Kelly family seemed like any other broken American family trying to move on. Geraldine "Geri" Kelly was a tough-as-nails mom who raised two kids largely on her own in the 1990s. She told everyone her husband – John – had died in a car accident. Tragic, yes, but sadly not uncommon. Geri and the children packed up their lives in California and moved back east to Massachusetts, settling into suburban obscurity. Neighbors in Somerville found Geri a bit odd perhaps (she had a penchant for tattoos, attack dogs, even wearing a pet snake as a scarf, according to those who knew her), but nothing could have prepared them for the bizarre truth lurking behind her storage unit door. Geri carried with her a *frozen* secret, one she kept locked up (literally) for 13 years: Her husband wasn't missing in action at all – he'd been chilling out in the freezer the whole time. Yes, you read that right. This devoted mother had been toting around a deep freezer containing her husband's corpse, like some morbid carry-on luggage, for over a decade. Talk about putting a marriage on ice.

It turns out Geri's marriage had been a nightmare of domestic violence behind closed doors. After years of abuse, one day in 1991 she decided she'd had enough. In a dramatic reversal of *'til death do us part*, she dealt John a terminal breakup via a gunshot to the back of his head. Problem solved? Not quite. Now she had a body on her hands – and Geri was nothing if not resourceful. She stashed John's remains in a chest freezer in their Ventura, California home. (We can only imagine her thought process: *"He wanted cold beer all the time; now he can be the cold one."*) When anyone asked, she spun a tale about him dying in a traffic accident, even telling the kids their dad had been "hit by a truck somewhere in Nevada". The audacity of that lie is almost artful – Nevada, of all places, as if he vanished into the desert like a bad casino bet. And for years, everyone bought it. After all, why would a seemingly loving wife and mother lie about such a thing?

Seven years passed. In 1998 Geri decided to relocate back to her hometown in Massachusetts, seeking a fresh start (or just new victims for her pet boa to scare). Here's where things cross from quirky into downright absurd: she had the moving company haul the freezer – still containing poor John's popsicle-like remains – across the country to Massachusetts. Picture the movers grunting and shoving this hefty freezer labeled "FRAGILE" into the truck, unknowingly transporting a literal *dead weight*. It sat in a Somerville storage facility for another six years, locked and sealed with duct tape – Geri's way of making sure her husband stayed *chilled out* and undiscovered. She even paid rental fees on that storage unit diligently. Talk about committing to a lie; most people won't keep a gym membership for 13 years, let alone a frozen corpse.

Over those years, Geri's relationship with her kids became strained. They were estranged by their late teens – perhaps rebellious angst, or maybe living with a human freezer in the house does something to the parent-child bond. Either way, they weren't exactly doing family game nights. And yet, the children never openly questioned the official story of Dad's fate. Geri was a master of the suburban secret: she stuck to her accident tale with iron-clad consistency. When the kids or relatives asked where John was buried, she deflected or refused to discuss it. (Red flag, anyone? "He's dead, but you don't need to know *where* he is" is not exactly a comforting answer. But denial is a powerful thing, and the family seems to have let it slide.)

It all unraveled in 2004. By then, Geri was gravely ill with breast cancer – karma coming to collect, some might say. From her hospital bed, sensing the icy fingers of mortality (no pun intended), she decided to unburden herself. In a dramatic deathbed mea culpa, Geri confessed to her adult daughter, "I killed your father. He's… well… in the freezer." One imagines the daughter's face went through all seven stages of shock in about two seconds. Geri justified her act by claiming years of spousal abuse drove her to it. Perhaps she hoped for understanding, even forgiveness, from her kids with that explanation. She then calmly provided the key detail: exactly where to find dear old dad's deep-frozen body. Shortly thereafter, having dropped this polar vortex of truth on her family, Geri passed away. (She always did have a flair for dramatic timing.)

What followed was a scene straight from a dark comedy crime show. Acting on the tip, police went to the local storage facility, likely expecting this might be some end-of-life delirium. Instead, they were greeted by the unmistakable odor of long-kept secrets. Inside the unit was the infamous freezer, still locked and sealed with layers of duct tape – Geri's DIY security system. Once opened, the "cold case" quite literally cracked wide: the remains of John Kelly, perfectly preserved like yesterday's leftovers, mummified from years on ice. They identified him easily from his distinctive tattoos – a panther, a Kewpie doll, a skull – still adorning his skin. It's not often police find a body in such *mint condition* after 13 years; for once, a murder victim was *literally* as cold as the case. Cause of death? Exactly what Geri had said – a close-range gunshot wound to the head, no ambiguity there.

The revelation sent ripples through both coasts. California folks who knew the couple at a Ventura motel they managed were slack-jawed that tough little Geri had harbored this nightmare all that time. In Massachusetts, the suburban gossip mill went into overdrive – suddenly those odd, standoffish Kelly kids had the most scandalous story in town. The cultural satire writes itself: behind the façade of even the most ordinary family, you might find *literal* skeletons in the freezer. Suburbia prides itself on manicured lawns and polite society, but as any true-crime fan knows, it's also the perfect habitat for secrets so absurd you'd think they were TV scripts. This one had all the tropes: the dutiful mom with a dark side, the missing spouse, the decades-long lie, and the final-hour confession that blows it all up. One could easily see a twisted episode of "Desperate Housewives" or a limited series on HBO inspired by Geri's saga (working title: "Cold Storage", of course).

Amidst the shock and horror, there's an element of dark humor in how the secret finally came out. Geri essentially said, "Surprise kids, the freezer you were told never to touch *was* your father all along. Love you, bye!" The absurdity is off the charts. Consider the freezer space priorities here: Geri literally prioritized preserving a corpse over, say, storing normal frozen goods. Imagine every time she felt like stocking up on ice cream or frozen pizzas, she had to think, "Nope, can't, John's taking up all the space." That's commitment to a cover-up – sacrificing your Ben & Jerry's for a secret. And hauling that heavy freezer cross-country? That's like a macabre twist on carrying a torch for someone; she carried the whole dang freezer. It gives new meaning to the phrase "keeping the family together." If this were a sitcom, there'd be a running gag of nosy neighbors asking why she never gets rid of that old freezer, and Geri offering a tight-lipped smile saying, "Oh, it's a family heirloom… very *dear* to me."

In the end, Geri's deathbed apology left her children with a tornado of emotions. There was relief – finally knowing what happened to Dad, no longer living with a question mark. There was anger and betrayal – their mother had lied to them their entire lives and let them believe a falsehood about their father's fate. There was even a weird kind of understanding from some quarters: Geri had been a battered woman who snapped, a tragic figure herself. The District Attorney mused aloud, unsure whether Geri confessed out of genuine remorse or simply to ensure her kids wouldn't be blamed if the body was found after her death. Perhaps it was both. In true performative style, Geri managed to cast herself in a martyr's light to the very end – *I endured abuse, I saved myself and you kids, I hid it to protect us, and I only tell you now to spare you trouble.* It's almost admirable in a twisted way: she controlled the narrative until the final act.

The absurdity of this family truth being revealed so late underscores a larger point: how well do we really know those closest to us? How many suburban smiles hide grim secrets to the grave? We chuckle at TV crime tropes – the husband in the freezer, the wife under the patio – thinking they're far-fetched, when real life says, "Hold my beer… and put it in the freezer next to Uncle John." The Kelly case invites us to laugh at the sheer outrageousness even as we recoil. It's a parody of domestic bliss: the ultimate "cold war" between spouses ending in an actual freeze. And it leaves a cautionary tale that family estrangement sometimes has very concrete causes (in this case, 180 pounds of cause kept on ice).

Moral: Secrets have a shelf life, even in the freezer. Eventually, the truth will defrost – and it's bound to make a stink when it does. In other words, you can put your problems on ice, but you can't stop them from perishing; so clean out your emotional freezer before it overflows with regret. Honesty may not be easy, but it sure beats hauling a deep-freeze of guilt through life (and across state lines).

8.4 An Unwilling Accomplice: The Redacted Revelations of Lady X

Scholars of crime history sometimes whisper about the mysterious case of Lady X, an upper-crust woman from a bygone era whose real identity remains concealed behind black bars in archival documents. Her story reads like an academic whodunit crossed with a soap opera. Lady X lived her life as a picture-perfect spouse to a prominent man – we'll call him Mr. Y – in the early 20th century. For decades, she was lauded as the supportive wife, a gracious hostess, a pillar of the community. Little did anyone suspect that she had played a small part in a big crime without even knowing it. It was only in her final hours, penning a shaky handwritten confession letter from her deathbed, that Lady X unraveled the secret she had unwittingly been keeping. What followed has fueled a century of academic controversy and satirical speculation about just how much *people choose to know or not know* when reputation is on the line.

According to the redacted letter (now preserved in a university library, with names and places blacked out like a classified spy file), Lady

X revealed that she had unknowingly abetted one of her husband's misdeeds. The crime in question? Historians deduce from context clues that it was a financial fraud scandal that rocked their city in the 1920s. Mr. Y, a charismatic businessman and local politician, was involved in embezzling a fortune – a detail that never made the society pages, thanks to a lack of evidence and perhaps some bribed officials. At the time, Lady X stood by him staunchly. She provided an *alibi*, swearing that on the night of the suspected embezzlement, Mr. Y was home with her, sick in bed. Her testimony helped quash suspicions and preserve their genteel standing. Case closed, high society none the wiser.

But in her deathbed letter, Lady X admitted a troubling truth: she had lied under oath *without realizing it*. That fateful night, she truly believed her husband was upstairs sleeping off an illness. In reality, as she discovered years later, he had slipped out and committed the deed while she dozed by the hearth. Unwittingly, she had given him the perfect cover. How did she eventually find out? The letter suggests that decades on, an attack of conscience (Mr. Y's conscience, that is) led him to confess to her in private – long after the statute of limitations and long after society had forgotten the entire affair. He begged her forgiveness, and being the dutiful wife, she kept his secret to the grave. Well, almost to the grave. Only when *she* lay dying did she decide to set the record straight, perhaps to make sure history wouldn't remember her as complicit in silence. It's juicy stuff: part mystery, part morality play. However, because the names were redacted "to protect the innocent" (or more likely the not-so-innocent descendants), scholars have had a field day debating which high-society couple this really was. It's like a parlor game for PhDs – there's even a theory tying Lady X to a famous 1920s banking family, though no one can say for sure.

The real intrigue here isn't just the crime, but the psychology. Lady X's story drips with satirical commentary about selective memory and plausible deniability among the elite. For years, she genuinely – or *conveniently* – remembered nothing amiss. Selective memory is a powerful thing; we recall what we can live with and file away the rest in a drawer marked "ignore." It's possible that Lady X had her suspicions earlier but chose not to investigate. Maybe she noticed the mud on Mr. Y's boots that morning, or the strange disappearance of certain ledger books around that time. But when your entire identity is built around being the impeccable wife of a reputable man, rocking the boat isn't exactly appealing. So perhaps she subconsciously did what many have done in positions of uncomfortable truth: looked the other way and forgot. After all, ignorance is bliss – and in high society, bliss is preferable to scandal.

Her later confession reads almost as an act of reputation maintenance *from beyond the grave.* By writing that letter, Lady X managed to frame herself not as a complicit liar, but as an *unwilling accomplice* who simply didn't know better. It's a deft piece of image laundering. She basically said, "I *unknowingly* helped cover up my husband's crime, and I only realized my mistake much later." The subtext being: *Don't judge me too harshly, I was fooled by love!* One can't help but smirk at the timing – only when all the players were dead or dying did the truth come out, protecting the family name during those precious years when scandal would have actually mattered. It's as though she wanted to have her proverbial cake and eat it: enjoy a lifetime of respectability and *then* clear her conscience right at the end, when it cost her nothing. How terribly convenient... and utterly human.

This case has prompted many an eye-roll and knowing chuckle among commentators. It mirrors the classic modern scene of a politician's spouse at a press conference, standing by with a strained smile, later claiming, "I had no idea what was going on behind closed doors." We've seen governors' wives, celebrity partners, and CFOs all singing from that hymnal of plausible deniability when scandal hits. Lady X was their protoype. She pioneered the art of the belated truth, revealing things only when it's too late for questions. There's even a whiff of *Oscar Wilde*-style satire here: the important thing in life is to have a clean reputation – if reality doesn't cooperate, just delay the truth until it's socially irrelevant.

Of course, not everyone buys Lady X's innocent act. Some historians argue she knew all along and only confessed to ease her guilty conscience, painting herself as naive to save face. Others believe her, citing her previously unblemished character and the genuine remorse evident in her writing. The debate gets heated in academic journals – one went so far as to title an article *"Guilty By Ignorance: The Ethics of Unknowing Accomplices."* The case of Lady X forces us to ask: how much *not knowing* is willful? At what point does blind trust become moral blindness? In her letter, Lady X grappled with these very questions. She wrote (paraphrasing), "I see now that my love and trust in my husband made me an instrument of his wrongdoing. I was a fool in my devotion." In her own flowery, early-

1900s way, she basically called herself out for being *too good at not asking questions*. It's a surprisingly self-aware admission, if a tad late.

The satirical element practically writes itself. One could imagine a stage play where Lady X's ghost narrates from the afterlife, sipping tea and tossing shade at her younger self: *"My dear, those pearls might be fake — much like your ignorance of your husband's midnight excursions."* There's also a lesson here about the performative nature of virtue in certain circles. Lady X likely prided herself on being the ideal wife, and that performance required turning a blind eye to unpleasant truths. It's a dance many have danced: keep the face powder dry while the cracks form underneath. Her deathbed confession is like the final act of that performance — a last soliloquy to the audience, revealing the truth and pleading for understanding.

In a broader context, Lady X's tale is a reminder of how history often has hidden accomplices. Behind many a notorious figure is someone in the shadows saying, "Who, me? I had *no idea!*" Perhaps they didn't at the time, or perhaps they just found it expedient not to. As a culture, we're simultaneously drawn to and suspicious of these claims of ignorance. We side-eye the mafia wife who never wondered why there was so much cash in the freezer (looking at you, real-life crime families). We raise eyebrows at the executive's partner who enjoyed the yachts and mansions but never pondered the sketchy accounting. Lady X stands as an early exemplar of that archetype — plausible deniability personified.

Moral: Truth has a way of surfacing, even if delivered with a delay and a dose of spin. It's a warning that turning a blind eye can make you an accessory *after the fact*, whether you intend it or not. In plainer terms: pretending not to know doesn't absolve you when the real story comes out – it just makes your eventual "oops, my bad" look a tad suspect. Better to face uncomfortable truths in the moment than to issue a posthumous press release to clear your name.

8.5 The Stolen Baby Revelation: Mom's Last Gift of Truth

Our final tale takes us into the thorny realm of parenthood, identity, and a secret that spent a lifetime under wraps. Meet a devoted mother – we'll call her Marie – who, for decades, played the role of Supermom with zeal. She baked cookies for the school bake sale, never missed a PTA meeting, and her house was the one on the block with the neat lawn and a wreath for every holiday. To neighbors and friends, Marie was the embodiment of wholesome suburban motherhood. She had one beloved daughter, whom she often called her "miracle baby." And indeed, the child was something of a miracle – but not in the way anyone thought. For over thirty years, Marie carried a secret so explosive it could blow up her carefully crafted world: her daughter was illegally obtained through a black-market baby trafficking ring.

It sounds like a plot from a daytime melodrama, but baby trafficking was (and is) a very real, if hushed, phenomenon. In the late 1970s, when Marie desperately wanted a child, adoption laws were stricter and societal pressures high. Rather than endure the scrutiny and waiting of legal adoption – or perhaps after being deemed "too old" or "unfit" by the standards of the day – Marie took a shortcut offered by a shady intermediary. Money quietly changed hands. One day she suddenly "had a baby" to bring home, no lengthy pregnancy or hospital stay required. To the outside world, she spun a tale: she and her husband had adopted a baby girl from a young mother who wished to remain anonymous. It had all been done privately, was her story, to spare everyone shame. In truth, her new daughter was sourced via an illegal network that arranged adoptions by *stealing or buying infants*. Marie knew on some level it was wrong – there were whispered phone calls, a furtive trip to another state to pick up the infant, and certainly no official paperwork beyond a falsified birth certificate. But she told herself that she was giving this child a good home, that this was her chance at motherhood, and that the *ends justified the means*. And so began her life as both a loving mom and a keeper of a colossal lie.

As the years rolled on, Marie poured her heart into raising her daughter. She was, by all accounts, a doting mother – the kind who would sew Halloween costumes by hand and show up to every dance recital with flowers. Perhaps overcompensating out of guilt, she made sure her daughter never doubted she was loved. However, there were signs of the secret if you knew where to look. Family photo albums conspicuously lacked any pictures of a pregnant Marie. When the curious child once asked, "Mom, did I grow in your tummy?", Marie froze and then deflected with a gentle fib about how *every* baby grows in their mommy's heart. Adoption was a taboo topic in their house, cloaked in half-truths and euphemisms. Marie walked a tightrope of *performative parenthood*, ever fearful that one slip could unravel everything. She became the president of an adoptive parents support group (oh, the irony) and loudly championed how *anyone* who raises a child is the "real" parent — a true statement, but in her case a deflection from the shady origin story.

Decades passed. The daughter grew into a kind, accomplished woman, crediting her mom's unwavering support for her success. But Marie's secret gnawed at her. Sometimes, late at night, she would take out the hidden file with the false papers and a single slip of paper bearing the name of her daughter's birth mother — a name she had never dared speak. She knew that somewhere out there was another woman who had carried this child and likely wondered for years what became of her baby. The weight of that stolen truth grew heavier as Marie grew older. And as tends to happen, the approach of one's final exit makes keeping such secrets less appealing. So, as Marie lay in hospice care, her body failing, she decided it was time for one last act of motherhood: telling the truth that would set her daughter free (and, incidentally, ease her own conscience).

In a tearful bedside confession, Marie revealed to her daughter the reality of her adoption. She explained how, as an infant, the daughter had been *procured* through illicit means — effectively trafficked — and that Marie had raised her under the pretense of a normal adoption. There were no violins playing, but the emotional wallop was immense. The daughter's world tilted on its axis. Imagine being in your 30s and learning not only that you were adopted (a shock if you hadn't known) but that it was done illegally, meaning your birth family hadn't willingly let you go. It's the kind of revelation that spawns both an identity crisis and an episode of *Law & Order: SVU*. Marie, sobbing, begged for forgiveness. She tried to explain the inexplainable: the desperation of childlessness that led her to break the law, the rationalizations she made that "you were loved and taken care of, that's what matters." She even attempted a bit of that old maternal martyrdom, saying, "I did it for you – to give you a good life." (A classic line from the Parental Justification Handbook, albeit here rather distorted: kidnapping by proxy *for your own good*.)

The daughter's reaction was a complex storm of emotions – love, anger, betrayal, compassion. On one hand, the woman she adored as her mother was now confessing to a crime that essentially founded their family. On the other, that woman was dying, clearly tormented by remorse, and still the same person who had been Mom in every meaningful way. This is the messy reality behind performative parenthood: sometimes the parent you idolize has a past that doesn't match the saintly image. It's as if Marie had been wearing a "World's Best Mom" t-shirt over a secret bulletproof vest of deception. Yet, in that moment, she stripped it all off, exposing herself as painfully human – flawed, selfish, loving, and sorry.

The cultural taboos around adoption and parenthood loomed large here. Marie had always feared the stigma: would people judge her for not being a "real" mother if they knew? Would her daughter feel less hers? Ironically, by hiding the truth, she guaranteed that the eventual discovery would be far more dramatic. It's a bit like the celebrity who desperately hides a scandal, only for it to explode when leaked – the Streisand Effect of family secrets. Modern pop culture has danced around similar themes (think of movies like *Philomena* or stories of stolen babies during dictatorships). In some countries, entire scandals have come to light of babies stolen and sold to unsuspecting (or willfully ignorant) adoptive parents. Marie's story could be one of those footnotes in a report about illegal adoptions in the 20th century. It underscores how something as beautiful as adopting a child can be twisted by black markets, and how those secrets fester within families.

After the big reveal, Marie's daughter did what many of us might: she sought answers and eventually forgiveness. Through a support network (and let's be honest, probably a therapist or two), she even managed to track down her biological roots. To Marie's relief, her daughter didn't reject her; rather, she added nuance to her understanding of "Mom." It was like discovering your favorite homemade pie had a strange ingredient – you're surprised and maybe a bit upset, but it's still the pie you loved all along, just with a more complicated recipe.

The satire in this saga lies in how Marie's life was an embodiment of performative virtue hiding a transgression. She made such a show of being the perfect mother that no one would suspect the imperfect beginnings. It's reminiscent of those politicians who champion family values while hiding secret families – eventually the truth tends to leak, often at the most inopportune time. At least Marie took control of the narrative at the end, giving her daughter the truth straight from the source instead of leaving her to find out via an errant 23andMe DNA test down the line (imagine that surprise in a crowded genealogy website forum). Indeed, one darkly comic aspect: if Marie hadn't confessed, modern consumer DNA kits very likely would have outed the secret in due time, with some random third cousin match revealing that the family tree branches didn't line up. In a sense, Marie beat technology to the punch.

As the dust settled, the family – now expanded in definition – found a sort of peace. Marie passed away with her daughter holding her hand, both of them in tears but bound by an unbroken bond of love, now laced with truth. The daughter later connected with her birth relatives, finding closure in learning her origin story (a mix of heartbreak and healing in its own right). It's not an ending tied in a neat bow, but life rarely is. The absurdity and profundity coexist: a mother's lie gave her a daughter, and that daughter's love gave the mother the courage to tell the truth.

Moral: Love built on a lie is still love – but a house of cards will eventually collapse under the weight of truth. In family matters, honesty truly is the best (and belated) policy. No matter how painful a secret is, bringing it to light can be a final act of love. Or to put it more cheekily: if you *do* have a long-lost secret, consider sharing it before the deathbed – it might save on shock-induced therapy bills later. In the grand tapestry of family dysfunction, transparency is the golden thread that can patch even the largest holes.

Chapter 9

Hoaxes Unveiled – Pranks, Frauds, and Final Comeuppance

9.1 Nessie's Hoax Exposed

The legend of the Loch Ness Monster was buoyed for decades by a single tantalizing photo – a grainy silhouette of a serpent-like neck rippling the Scottish waters, equal parts spooky and enchanting. This 1934 snapshot, known as the "Surgeon's Photograph," became the Kardashians of cryptid evidence – famous for being famous, plastered in papers and drawing tourists like a monster-themed Disneyland. It was the ultimate early-20th-century viral image, prompting countless family road trips to Loch Ness with Dad scanning the waves as eagerly as kids watching for Santa. Everyone from serious zoologists to pub regulars debated *Nessie's* existence with a fervor that today's Twitter conspiracists would admire.

Yet behind that iconic image lay not an ancient dinosaur, but a *toy submarine* playing dress-up. In a twist worthy of a soap opera finale, the fearsome Loch Ness Monster was outed as a mere model a mere 14 inches long – the product of an audacious prank. The plot was hatched by Marmaduke Wetherell, a big-game hunter nursing a bruised ego after a previous Nessie-hunting fiasco (involving some fake "monster" footprints that turned out to be made with a hippopotamus-foot umbrella stand – yes, really). To get revenge on the tabloids that had humiliated him, Wetherell conspired with his stepson, *Chris Spurling*, and others to craft a monster-on-demand. They cobbled together a Woolworth's submarine toy with a putty neck and headed to the loch for a photoshoot. Colonel Robert Wilson, a London surgeon with a respectable name, was roped in to sell the photo to the press (hence the picture's lasting title). The result? The world's most famous monster cameo – a prehistoric *peekaboo* that had the globe enthralled.

For a while, the hoax worked swimmingly. 1930s society was perhaps primed to believe in monsters; after all, King Kong was a box-office hit and news was rife with talk of dinosaurs and deep-sea beasts. The Loch Ness image splashed across headlines, *quite literally*, and Nessie became a superstar cryptid. In an era before Photoshop, a blurry photo felt like unassailable proof – as if the loch had said "cheese" and served up a sea serpent. Never mind that the "monster" in the shot was suspiciously well-behaved, always surfacing at photogenic moments and never, say, gobbling fishermen. Hopeful believers flocked to Loch Ness for years, straining to spot that familiar long neck in the misty waves. It was an early instance of influencer culture, 1930s style – Nessie had *influence* (on travel budgets and imaginations) despite being as real as a Hollywood prop. One could say Nessie was the original virtual influencer: an entity with millions of fans and zero actual substance.

The truth finally paddled ashore decades later. In 1994, on his deathbed, Chris Spurling at last blurted out the secret: *Surprise!* The Loch Ness Monster was a sham – a petite plastic plesiosaur, not a living dinosaur. The admission confirmed what some skeptics had long suspected and what every kid who grew up on Scooby-Doo learned eventually: often there's a meddling human behind the monster. Modern monster-hunters reacted with a mix of heartbreak and *"I knew it!"* eye-rolls. It was as if the Wizard of Oz's curtain had been yanked back, revealing a chuckling prankster where awe and fear had stood. The Loch's biggest celebrity was exposed as a fraud, and one could imagine Nessie slinking off into retirement, her image rights still earning Scotland's tourism a fortune.

Humor aside, the Nessie hoax's final comeuppance was oddly poetic. Here was a creature that never was – unmasked in the end by the very humans who created her myth. Yet, like any juicy rumor, the *idea* of Nessie had grown larger than the truth. Even after the toy submarine revelation, true believers shrugged, "Maybe the photo was fake, but Nessie *could* still be down there." In pubs around Loch Ness, old timers likely raised a glass to the monster's ghost, spinning new tales for the tourists. After all, why let facts sink a perfectly good story? The Loch Ness hoax showed that we sometimes *prefer* the entertaining lie over the boring truth – a phenomenon alive and well in the age of Instagram filters and fake news. Nessie's saga is a reminder that humanity's love for wonder can make us see what isn't there, and sometimes it takes a wooden-necked toy to teach us the difference.

9.2 Séance Sisters Come Clean

The Fox sisters – Maggie and Kate – were the OG ghostbusters of the 19th century, except they were more adept at busting gullibility than ghosts. Picture two cheeky young girls in 1848 upstate New York, bored at bedtime, deciding it would be hilarious to convince the grown-ups their house was haunted. It started innocently: a stolen apple tied to a string, bouncing on the floor in the dark to mimic spectral knocks. When that got old, they graduated to cracking their knuckles and toes under the covers, producing eerie *rap-tap-taps* that spooked their naïve parents and neighbors. To any parent now dealing with kids who fake Wi-Fi outages to avoid homework, the Fox sisters' prank sounds adorably amateur – but in their time, it was the equivalent of a TikTok stunt gone massively viral.

Word spread, curiosity mounted, and soon the sisters had an audience. Enter big sister Leah, with a glint of dollar signs in her eyes, essentially becoming the Victorian era's most enterprising "momager." She whisked Maggie and Kate off to Rochester and beyond, charging people to witness the mysterious rappings from beyond. In a few short years, the teenage Fox girls went from playing pretend in a farmhouse to headlining séance shows for hundreds of paying customers. They were spiritualist superstars, the Billie Eilish of bump-in-the-night entertainment, with newspapers dubbing their act the real deal. Never mind that some skeptics correctly guessed the girls were cracking joints to make the sounds – many others *desperately wanted* to believe. This was mid-1800s America, a time when séances were as trendy as today's VR headsets, and the Fox sisters were at the center of the craze.

For context, the sisters' rise paralleled the explosion of the Spiritualism movement – a sort of religious fad where contacting the dead was all the rage. It was an age of earnest belief in invisible forces; even celebrities of the era (like First Lady Mary Todd Lincoln) dabbled in séances. The Foxes, with their girlish charm and inexplicable rappings, became the movement's poster children. They were influencers before Instagram – only instead of hawking detox tea, they peddled hope of an afterlife connection. Imagine a dim parlor room: wide-eyed attendees holding hands, the Fox sisters solemnly asking "Spirit, are you with us?" *Knock-knock-knock!* Cue gasps. It was part performance art, part collective therapy for a grieving culture. And it *worked*. People left convinced they'd touched the beyond, when really they'd only heard the well-timed pop of a teenage toe joint.

But as any content creator can tell you, keeping up a charade can be exhausting – and the Fox girls paid a price. By the 1880s, both Maggie and Kate struggled with alcoholism, burdened by years of fame and perhaps guilt (or at least, sibling drama exacerbated by spirits of the liquid kind). Their relationship with sister Leah frayed; they felt exploited, and she felt unappreciated. Finally, Maggie had enough. In 1888, four decades after the prank that sparked a religion, she blew the whistle in spectacular fashion. At New York's Academy of Music, before a live audience and eager reporters, Maggie Fox *came clean*. She revealed the rapping's mundane origins – the apples on strings, the cracking toes – even taking off her shoe on stage to demonstrate the toe trick for all to witness. One moment the crowd was laughing at the absurdity; the next they shuddered at how *weirdly* unsettling it was that this widow in black could summon such sounds from her foot on a wooden stool. "There stood a black-robed, sharp-faced widow…working her big toe" a newspaper reported, calling the scene "one moment ludicrous, the next weird". If there had been Twitter in 1888, #ToeTruth would have trended worldwide.

Maggie's public confession was a bombshell. Here were the founding sisters of Spiritualism admitting it was all "a horrible deception" from their childhood on. The press declared it "the death blow" to the movement. High-profile believers were mortified; the *Spiritual Telegraph*'s former publisher literally tried to ghost-splain Maggie's recantation by saying evil spirits *made* her fake it (an early example of conspiracy theorists moving goalposts!). Indeed, even after the sisters' hoax was unveiled, many die-hards refused to accept the truth. Spiritualism chugged along, undeterred – a case study in confirmation bias: people believe what they *want* to believe, facts be damned. The Fox sisters themselves later wavered; faced with public scorn and likely financial pressures, Maggie at one point tried to walk back her confession, but the cat (or ghost) was out of the bag.

In the end, the final comeuppance for the Fox sisters was bittersweet. They had kick-started a cultural phenomenon and then lived to see it spiral beyond their control. By confessing, they sacrificed their last shreds of fame (and income), effectively canceling themselves in an era with no rehab for disgraced mediums. The two younger sisters died poor and largely ostracized, whereas Leah – who perhaps always believed in the power of a good show over truth – died earlier, comfortably. It's a story with modern echoes: siblings pull a viral prank, ride the fame, then face backlash when the truth outs. Think of YouTube pranksters who admit their stunts were staged – their followers express shock, some anger, but a good chunk just move on to the next bizarre thing. The Fox saga reveals a timeless insight: we often *collude* in our own deception. The sisters tugged at America's gullible funny bone, and America, bereaved and hopeful, *let itself be fooled.* Family mischief rarely had such far-reaching consequences. And when Maggie Fox wiggled her toe on that stage, exposing the mechanism behind the miraculous, it was a moment of sharp, almost comedic clarity – the kind that makes you slap your forehead and chuckle, "Of course it was just that!" even as you feel a pang of loss for the beautiful lie that it toppled.

9.3 Fairy Tale Fess-Up

In the summer of 1917, two schoolgirl cousins in Yorkshire pulled off a hoax so fanciful that it snared the imagination of none other than Sherlock Holmes' creator – and if *that* isn't a plot twist, what is? Sixteen-year-old Elsie Wright and nine-year-old Frances Griffiths were the masterminds behind the Cottingley Fairies, a series of five photographs purporting to show real winged fairies flitting around their garden. One famous shot (see above) shows Elsie seated by a glen, serenely smiling at a capering one-foot-tall gnome like she's Snow White having tea with the dwarfs. In another, Frances poses with delicate fairies dancing in the air. These photos are quaint and slightly absurd by today's standards – the fairies look like paper cut-outs (which, spoiler, they were) – yet in an era bloodied by World War I, they were the *exact* escapist magic people craved. Think of it as the original Instagram filter: a touch of sparkle and fantasy over gritty reality, and oh, how everyone wanted to believe it was authentic.

The girls hadn't set out to fool the world. Initially, it was a lark to mess with the grown-ups – a bit of imaginative play with Elsie's father's camera. Elsie, a talented artist, sketched dainty fairy figures on paper, trimmed them out, and propped them up with hatpins amid the Cottingley woods. Frances would then pose with these sprite cut-outs, both girls doing their best to look astonished at the pixie revelry around them while trying not to giggle. When the first photographs were developed, even Elsie's skeptical father had to admit the images were striking, if suspiciously crisp. But Elsie's mother was a believer in *Theosophy* (a kind of spiritualist movement), so when she saw the photos, she immediately thought, "Aha! Proof of nature spirits!" In a perfect storm of credulity, she took the images to a meeting of the Theosophical Society. There, the photos caught the eye of a true heavyweight believer: Sir Arthur Conan Doyle. Yes, the man who gave the world the ultra-rational Sherlock Holmes was himself a spiritualist yearning for evidence of the unseen. To him, these fairy pictures were like a godsend – literally. He published them in the Christmas 1920 issue of *The Strand Magazine* alongside a glowing article about the existence of fairies. Boom! The photos went viral (in a 1920s way – i.e., they got a lot of press and cocktail party chatter).

Suddenly, the Cottingley cousins found themselves in the eye of a media storm. Imagine the pressure: one minute you're mucking about in the garden, the next you're the subject of international debate. Scientists examined the photos; photography experts like those at Kodak said, "Well, the negatives show no obvious tampering" (which was true – the images were straight-up photos of fake fairies). Skeptics pointed out the fairies looked suspiciously like illustrations from popular books (they were; Elsie copied them from a children's book, wings and all). But many people, including Doyle, so *wanted* it to be true that they explained away any doubts. Conan Doyle, who was apparently all-in on this whimsy, remained a staunch defender and believed in the fairies to his dying day – he never lived to see the hoax revealed and likely went to the grave imagining a whole hidden Fairyland in Yorkshire. This is a bit like if J.K. Rowling today earnestly believed in photos of a real-life Tinker Bell and missed the memo that it was just two kids and some paper dolls.

As the decades passed, the fame of the Cottingley Fairies lingered like a catchy song. The photos were reprinted in books and discussed in whatever was the early 20th-century equivalent of Reddit threads. All the while, Elsie and Frances grew up, got married, had real lives. They mostly kept their secret, perhaps out of embarrassment or a sense that the truth would disappoint too many people – or maybe because no one likes admitting they duped Sherlock Holmes' dad. Family gatherings must have been interesting: did they ever wink and nudge when someone brought up fairies? By the 1980s, both cousins were elderly, and the jig, perhaps, was up. In 1983, with skepticism about the photos growing, Elsie and Frances finally fessed up in print: yes, the fairy photos were fake. All of them? reporters asked. The ladies – still cheeky after all those years – maintained that while *four* of the photos were staged, one last photo was *possibly real*. (Even in confession, they left a sprinkle of fairy dust.) Frances swore that the fifth photograph, depicting ethereal fairy sunbathers, was genuine and that she had actually seen fairies that day. Elsie politely disagreed, asserting it was fake like all the rest. This absurd little family squabble over which fake fairy was *maybe* real is the kind of epilogue that makes the whole tale even more charmingly human. It's as if they couldn't quite let go of *all* the magic, having lived with it for so long.

The public's reaction to the confession was a collective, "Wait, you mean to tell us that those clearly illustrated fairies weren't legit? Shocking!" Cue laughter. By 1983, the world had seen the likes of Star Wars special effects and Photoshop was on the horizon – fooling people with paper fairies seemed endearingly quaint. If anything, the revelation only enhanced the Cottingley story's legend: it became a cautionary tale of how easily wishful thinking can triumph over logic. It's a story we see echoed today whenever a fake viral video makes the rounds (how many times have we seen "real mermaid caught on camera!" on YouTube, only to find it's CGI?). The Cottingley fairies, however, stand out because of the players involved – two mischievous girls and a credulous famous author – and because the hoax lasted so long. Their final comeuppance was gentle; by coming clean themselves, Elsie and Frances largely escaped the harsher judgment others have faced. In fact, many applauded them for their creativity. Frances in her later years even mused that they never expected people to take it so seriously – to them it was just a bit of fun that got wonderfully out of hand.

In retrospect, the Cottingley fairy hoax feels almost wholesome. Two kids with wild imaginations gave the world a fairy tale when it desperately needed one, and decades later as grandmothers they said, essentially, *"Gotcha! But wasn't it lovely?"* Their prank-to-publication pipeline prefigures today's influencer culture, where a random teenager's TikTok can captivate millions with a clever illusion. The difference is, now we are far more cynical – or at least savvy – about what we see. Yet, the Cottingley story reminds us that even smart adults (looking at you, Conan Doyle) can be *total suckers* for a beautiful lie. And perhaps that's not entirely a bad thing. We all perform a little suspension of disbelief when we watch a Marvel movie or when our children earnestly host an "invisible tea party" with imaginary friends. The Cottingley cousins simply played an unusually successful round of make-believe with the whole world. Their eventual confession closed the chapter with a wink, ensuring their tale lives on as a charming parable: sometimes people see what they want to see – especially if what they want to see is fairies at the bottom of the garden.

9.4 Bigfoot's Biggest Hoaxer

Behold Bigfoot, the hairy superstar of peekaboo photography, striding through a Northern California clearing in 1967 – or so this famous film frame would have us believe. For decades, Sasquatch was the king of cryptids in North America: a legend of a burly, camera-shy wildman leaving behind only blurry photos, enormous footprints, and the occasional petrified camper. But what if the *biggest* thing about Bigfoot was not the creature, but the whopper of a hoax that launched his fame? Enter Ray L. Wallace, a logging contractor with a prankster's heart, who can fairly be called the P.T. Barnum of Bigfoot. In 1958, in Humboldt County, California, Wallace orchestrated the prank that effectively birthed "Bigfoot" as we know it.

It started innocently enough (as these things often do): Wallace and his crew found giant, mysterious footprints around their work site – huge humanoid tracks that seemingly appeared out of nowhere in the muddy ground. Cue the "X-Files" music! Local newspapers ran the story, dubbing the unknown track-maker "Bigfoot," and a legend was born. Of course, what the papers didn't know was that Wallace himself had planted the prints, using a pair of cunningly carved 16-inch wooden feet strapped to his boots. It was literally *Bigfoot cosplay*, done as a practical joke on his co-workers. Wallace later chuckled that the first guy who saw the fake prints "just freaked out" – mission accomplished for a jokester. The story went national, feeding a growing appetite for mysterious creatures (this was the Cold War; people were into aliens and unknown species, perhaps as a diversion). Rather than fess up, Wallace did what any self-respecting trickster would: he doubled down.

Over the ensuing years, he became a one-man Bigfoot content farm. Wallace reported Bigfoot sightings whenever it suited him; he played pre-recorded "Bigfoot howls" from the woods to spook people; he even trotted out plaster casts of giant footprints like souvenirs. As his son Michael later quipped, Ray Wallace "played the faithful like a violin and giggled behind his hand the whole time". This man was essentially running a long-con reality show where he was the producer, Bigfoot was the star (and also imaginary), and the audience was *everyone*. And what an audience it was – the Bigfoot myth caught fire. Other folks hopped on the bandwagon, reporting their own Sasquatch encounters in the Pacific Northwest and beyond. It became a pop-culture phenomenon: you had cheesy Bigfoot B-movies, "real" Bigfoot hair samples (usually deer or bear fur), and pseudo-documentaries with earnest investigators creeping through forests whispering, "Did you hear that?" By the late 1960s, we got the Patterson–Gimlin film (from which the above image is taken), arguably the most famous Bigfoot footage of all, which many suspect was also a hoax – just not one of Wallace's making. Bigfoot had evolved into the Kim Kardashian of cryptids – famous, elusive, and on magazines everywhere despite a perplexing lack of concrete reason.

Ray Wallace, meanwhile, watched with amusement as his private joke went global. He never publicly took credit during his lifetime, perhaps enjoying the chaos too much to spoil it. It wasn't until 2002, upon Wallace's death at age 84, that his family finally spilled the beans. "There wasn't enough room in Ray's grave for him and his hoax, so now the truth is out: Bigfoot didn't exist – or at least not the Bigfoot that Wallace helped make famous," wrote the Los Angeles Times in a cheeky obituary. Wallace's children revealed the old man had a garage full of evidence: those crudely carved wooden feet, a map of where he left prints, and a gleeful knowledge of the prank's success. They recounted how their dad had essentially spent decades privately howling with laughter as scientists, hunters, and late-night TV hosts obsessed over his myth. "He was a prankster, but never malicious," his son Michael said. "He just liked playing jokes". In fact, growing up Wallace sounded kind of fun – the family recounts pet cougars and skunks in their home, and endless practical jokes as dinner table fodder. One can imagine a young Michael Wallace at school, bragging, "My dad *is* Bigfoot," and everyone taking it as a metaphor.

The reaction to the Wallace confession was mixed comedy and cognitive dissonance. Serious Bigfoot researchers (yes, they exist) weren't *too* fazed; many had long suspected some of the evidence was hoaxed. Some even shrugged it off, saying Wallace's tracks were just one chapter and that the "real Bigfoot" could still be out there – the classic conspiracy theorist pivot. Indeed, an Idaho anthropologist noted that while Wallace's antics could be behind a lot of it, he wasn't ready to toss all Bigfoot lore out the window. True believers gonna believe – even when you show them the wooden shoes that started it all, they'll say, "Well, those prints, sure, but *what about* that other sighting?" It's basically the Flat Earth mentality: one piece of debunking just leads them to cling tighter to what's left.

Still, the image of Ray Wallace's final laugh is enduring. The man pulled off a legendary hoax that became a cultural icon, and he lived to see Bigfoot enter the pantheon of modern mythology – probably winking slyly the whole time. His final comeuppance, if you can call it that, was that *everyone finally knew he'd been laughing at them*. But by then, Bigfoot was bigger than one man; the creature had taken on a life of its own, marching through our collective imagination with giant footprints that no longer belonged to Wallace or anyone. In a sense, Wallace succeeded *too* well – he created an idea that escaped his control. Today, we still see Bigfoot plastered on bumper stickers, prowling through beef jerky commercials, and headlining reality TV specials. The hoax that Ray built has become a multi-million-dollar industry of tours, merchandise, and folklore. As hoaxes go, Bigfoot is less a cautionary tale and more of an ode to human credulity and love of mystery. And maybe also an ode to the prankster spirit – the part of us that wants to spin a good yarn and the part of us that wants desperately for that yarn to be true. Ray Wallace managed to tickle both, and somewhere up in heaven (or Bigfoot Valhalla), you can bet he's still giggling about it.

9.5 Circles in the Corn

If aliens ever visit Earth, they might be perplexed to learn that two mischievous English blokes once fooled a whole lot of humans into thinking extraterrestrials had a fetish for landscaping. The phenomenon of crop circles – those elaborate geometric patterns that mysteriously began appearing in English grain fields in the late 1970s – had the world's minds whirring. Were they landing pads for UFOs? Secret military experiments? Messages from Gaia? For years, every summer brought new formations etched in wheat or corn overnight, as if some cosmic gardener had gone on a bender with a protractor. New Agers rejoiced, farmers grumbled, and scientists scratched their heads. And through it all, *no one knew* who (or what) was behind the spectacle… until 1991, when the curtain fell. That year, two amiable retirees from Southampton – Doug Bower and Dave Chorley – stepped forward, grins on their faces and wooden planks in hand, to announce: *"It was us, mates."*

Yes, the entire global mystery was the work of a couple of 60-something pranksters armed with nothing more exotic than ropes, boards, and a good old dose of English cheek. It turns out Doug and Dave had been making these flattened crop designs since 1978 as a private joke, inspired by tales of a "flying saucer nest" in Australia and fueled by many a pint at their local pub. They started with simple circles

— just a couple of lads having a laugh in a wheat field — and when those rudimentary crop circles hit the news and people went wild with speculation, they thought, why not *up our game?* Over the next decade, their designs became larger and more intricate, as if challenging the growing ranks of "cereologists" (the fancy term for crop circle researchers) to keep pace. The more scientists and paranormal buffs insisted "No mere mortal could bend corn so precisely!" the more Doug and Dave upped the ante, devising ever more complex patterns to shout, "Oh yes we can!". It was like a secret competition: the duo versus the experts, with the rest of us as clueless spectators.

By the late 1980s, crop circles had spread beyond Britain, popping up in fields from the US to Japan, and theories about their origin grew wilder than the patterns themselves. You had UFO true-believers, of course, and folk claiming vortex energy or Gaia's communications. Tourist buses were doing crop-circle circuits, and souvenir t-shirts were selling like hotcakes in affected towns. Meanwhile, Doug and Dave were watching their anonymous art project spiral out of control — and other copycats were jumping in, making circles of their own. It reached a point where our two original hoaxers feared they might take the secret to their graves without any credit (or blame). Plus, Doug's wife had started noticing suspicious mileage on the car each morning and wondered if he was having an affair — imagine her face when he confessed the only other woman in his life was Lady Barley of Wiltshire! In fact, it was this domestic friction that finally pushed the pair to *come clean.* As Bower explained, "We're not getting any younger," and they didn't fancy their legacy being stolen by either rumor or those darned UFOs. They contacted a London paper, Today, and arranged a demonstration. In front of journalists, Doug and Dave stomped out a classic circle in a Kent field in minutes flat, using just their low-tech tools and a heck of a lot of experience. The reporters then brought a well-known circle "expert" to see the freshly made pattern. He examined the crushed stalks, pronounced (with absolute conviction) that "no human being" could have made such perfect circles and that it must be the work of a high mysterious force. Talk about *awkward* – the journalists then introduced the very human circle-makers, like a prank reality show reveal. The poor expert exclaimed, "We have been conned. This is a dirty trick!" yet, hilariously, even after being shown the truth, he *still* couldn't fully accept it. By the next day, he was denying the hoax and insisting there was more to the phenomenon. You can't make this stuff up – well, actually Dave and Doug did, and how.

When the story broke publicly, it was a global sensation. Many were amused that two pensioners had hoodwinked the world (score one for the old-timers!). Others were crestfallen; believers in alien artistry clung desperately to the idea that *some* circles might still be paranormal (surely E.T. did the one with the really fancy swirls!). But the evidence was undeniable: Bower and Chorley claimed responsibility for around 2000 circles over 13 years, covering most of the major formations in England, and they even showed off their original sketch maps of designs. They revealed how they managed to stay undetected: working in the dead of night, using existing tractor trails to avoid leaving footprints, and having a few close calls with curious passersby that only added to the adrenaline. One time, they heard a group of locals approaching the field and had to hide lying down in the crops, stifling laughter as the onlookers marveled at the "UFO landing site" not realizing the artists were literally at their feet.

Perhaps the funniest twist is the jealousy and annoyance that drove the confession. Doug and Dave were miffed that while they remained in the shadows, others were cashing in on *their* prank. Authors like Pat Delgado (the expert above) were selling bestsellers about crop circles being the work of aliens or Mother Earth's energies. New circle-makers were doing copycat patterns elsewhere, and our duo grumbled, *some of those newbies do sloppy work*. In short, D&D wanted recognition – the prank had outgrown its original intent and become an unpaid second career! As Chorley quipped about the true believers still in denial, "If they want to go on with the charade, that is up to them". It was the mic-drop moment of one of history's great hoaxes.

In the aftermath, crop circles didn't disappear – the genie was out of the bottle. Instead, they transformed. A new generation of "circle-makers" treated it as a form of land art. Some did it for fun, others for profit; companies hired teams to create crop circle ads (everything from Pringles crisps to Firefox logos appeared in fields). Meanwhile, hardcore cereologists concocted ever more baroque rationalizations: maybe *some* circles are human-hoaxed but the *real* ones are still unexplained – a classic no-true-Scotsman fallacy, or rather, no-true-crop-circle. For Doug and Dave, however, the jig was delightfully up. Their final act – stepping into the spotlight – gave them a taste of the fame they had anonymously cultivated. One might say their final comeuppance was realizing the power of their art only after revealing themselves. They got a few late-in-life years of celebrity, appearing on talk shows with their planks, merrily demonstrating circle-making for incredulous audiences. And when asked why they did it, their answer was essentially, *"For the fun, of course!"* There's something heartwarming about that. Two friends with a shared sense of humor managed to prank the world, spark a cultural phenomenon, and then bow out with a humble brag and a chuckle.

The crop circle caper illuminates a bigger truth about human nature: We often prefer a wondrous lie to a boring truth. Even when the hoaxers are literally *in the field* showing how it's done, some will squint at the sky and whisper, "Those clever aliens!" But it also shows how innovation and mischief can go hand in hand. Doug and Dave didn't have college degrees or high-tech gadgets — they had creativity and corn stalks. In a way, they were artists who never expected their canvases to be viewed by millions. Their legacy lives on every time a new crop design pops up and people scratch their heads. And if you listen carefully on a quiet English summer night, you might almost hear two old men laughing in the distance, the echoes of the greatest cornfield prank in history.

Chapter 10

Grave Humor – Oddball Confessions and Final Laughs

It's often said that the truth comes out in the end – but nobody said it couldn't come out with a punchline. There's something oddly human about saving our strangest confessions and miscommunications for the final moments. In families everywhere, prankish grandparents and silent great-aunts carry secrets to their graves, only to toss out a curveball just before the curtain falls. This chapter is a journey through a handful of these bizarre last-act revelations. We'll meet relatives who spent decades trapped in misunderstandings of their own making, elders who delivered one last zinger, and loved ones left scratching their heads (or digging up backyards) for answers. All together, these oddball confessions shine a light on our penchant for mischief, miscommunication, and unspoken truths – even in life's final moments.

10.1 The Owl Obsession That Never Was

For half a century, one grandmother's home looked like an owl sanctuary meets antique shop. Picture a cozy living room absolutely overrun by owls – figurines, pillows, cookie jars. If it had big round eyes and feathers, she owned it. Every birthday and Christmas, without fail, her well-meaning family gifted her something owl-themed. By the time she was pushing ninety, she had amassed thousands of owl trinkets over the years. Friends joked that walking into her house felt like stepping into an Etsy search page for "owl decor."

The family was absolutely convinced she adored owls. After all, why else would she have so many? They never realized they were the ones who had started and then fed this owl craze. It began innocently enough, decades ago. Grandma bought one little owl trivet for her kitchen — just a casual purchase. A relative saw it and exclaimed, *"She must love owls!"* Cue the avalanche of owl gifts. One owl item led to another, and soon owls flowed like wine into every corner of her life.

Now, Grandma was a gracious lady. Every time she unwrapped yet another owl figurine or owl-themed cardigan, she mustered a smile and a thank you. By the time it got ridiculous, she figured it was too late to correct anyone. She might even have found it amusing. So she played along, living in an unintended owl museum – perhaps hoping someone might eventually ask, "Grandma, do you *really* like owls?" (Spoiler: no one did.)

It wasn't until she was 98 years old, lying in a hospital bed, that this lifelong misunderstanding finally unraveled. At 98, on her deathbed, her family finally asked if she had any last confessions. She paused, then sighed and uttered: "I never understood the owls." With that one sentence, decades of pretense melted away. She confessed she didn't actually give a hoot about owls — literally, *did not give a hoot*. For a moment the room was silent – then everyone burst into laughter, realizing the entire owl saga had been one big misunderstanding.

Grandma's last-minute admission was delivered with impeccable comedic timing – a final gift of laughter to her family. In that absurd moment they learned: if you don't actually love something, speak up before you drown in it. The family, chagrined but amused, gained a running joke for generations. Grandma had endured a 50-year owl invasion with a twinkle in her eye, only revealing the truth when it would get the biggest laugh. To this day, the family can't see an owl without cracking up. They still send each other owl memes captioned "I never understood the owls."

10.2 The Great Meatball Hoax

Every family has that one signature dish that holds almost mythical status. In our next tale, Grandpa's Sicilian meatballs were the stuff of legend. These meatballs were said to be so good they could make a stoic man weep. At every big family dinner, when his platter of meatballs would appear, everyone dug in eagerly and fought for the last one. Grandpa – a jolly fellow in an apron reading "Kiss the Cook" – would just smile and say, "Ah, the secret is the love I put in it." Since he emigrated from Sicily as a young man, everyone assumed these were authentic, passed-down-for-generations Sicilian meatballs seasoned by old-country wisdom.

For decades, Grandpa played the role of master chef to perfection. He'd spend all day "making the sauce" and insist on the freshest ingredients. Grandkids who wandered into the kitchen would see him humming Sinatra over a simmering pot. The aromas alone were the definition of comfort. He never let anyone watch him mix the meatballs.

"It's an old family recipe, molto secret," he'd joke with a wink. To the younger ones, his cooking seemed almost mystical.

But Grandpa's greatest recipe turned out to be an epic recipe for *deception*. Fast forward to his twilight years. In his final days, with his family gathered around (perhaps already planning to honor his memory by publishing "Grandpa's Famous Meatballs" in a cookbook), he decided it was time for the truth. With a weak but mischievous grin, he confessed: "About those meatballs… they're actually the frozen kind from the supermarket." Cue stunned silence, then disbelieving chuckles. Surely, Nonno must be kidding? The man who taught them the value of fresh herbs and a pinch of this and that from the heart – serving frozen meatballs?

He *wasn't* kidding. He went on to explain that long ago, as a busy young dad, he'd discovered a decent frozen meatball brand and doctored it up with his own sauce and seasonings. One day his boss was coming to dinner, so in a pinch he threw those pre-made meatballs in the pot. Everyone raved about them and assumed he'd hand-rolled them from veal and pork like a true Sicilian *nonna*. Grandpa was tickled and just never corrected them. "If it ain't broke, don't fix it," he wheezed with a laugh. His pride in being the family's beloved chef had started as a little white lie that snowballed. Once the myth took hold, he rode that wave for 40 years. Why disappoint everyone (including himself) by revealing the truth?

The family's reaction was a mix of uproarious laughter and a bit of scandalized shock. One son even clutched his chest in mock betrayal, crying, "My life is a lie!" The story became an instant classic in the family. Memes of a Scooby-Doo unmasking ("Let's see who you REALLY are!") captioned "Grandpa's secret ingredient" circulated, keeping everyone laughing through their tears.

The great meatball hoax taught the family an important, if humorous, lesson about honesty and the power of a good story. They realized they hadn't loved Grandpa for his cooking at all – they loved him for the warmth and joy he brought to the table. The meatballs, real or fake, were just an excuse to gather. At his memorial, the family even served – you guessed it – frozen meatballs in his honor, complete with a sign reading "Homemade (sort of)." In the end, his true secret ingredient really was love (with a dash of playful deceit).

10.3 The Mystery of the Seventeen Orange Tennis Balls

Some confessions don't bring closure or clarity – they create a riddle that haunts those left behind. Take the peculiar case of the dying man and the seventeen orange tennis balls. For years, this gentleman harbored a bizarrely specific wish: he wanted exactly 17 bright orange tennis balls. Not 10, not 20 – seventeen on the dot – and specifically orange, not the usual neon yellow. It became a running joke in the family. Every birthday, if you asked what he wanted, he'd grin and say, "17 orange tennis balls." Most relatives just shrugged it off as a harmless quirk – like collecting all the state quarters. Honestly, a fixation on tennis balls seemed pretty benign.

Still, over the years the family's curiosity quietly grew. Occasionally, someone would ask, "But… why 17? And why orange?" Each time, the old man would just smile mysteriously and wave it off. Did he plan to juggle them? Was it a secret code? One grandson jokingly theorized that Grandpa had buried treasure and marked the spot with those orange balls. Whatever the reason, it remained an unresolved mystery – the kind of weird family lore that would make a great viral Reddit thread titled "Grandpa won't tell us why he needs 17 orange tennis balls, and it's driving us nuts!"

The answer, apparently, was destined to be revealed dramatically. In his final moments, surrounded by family, he finally decided to explain the truth behind the tennis balls. You can imagine everyone perking up, leaning in eagerly. This was it – the finale to a lifelong puzzle. With a frail voice, he began to reveal the secret: "All these years, all I ever asked for was seventeen orange tennis balls. Now, at the end of my life, I can finally tell you all why I needed them. You see, back when I was in my twenties, I found out—" And then he died, mid-sentence. Just like that.

The family was left in disbelief – and, to their own shame, a touch of dark amusement at the absurdity. As the heart monitor flatlined, one of his kids blurted out, "Are you *serious*?!" (then sheepishly apologized to the nurse). They'd been *so close* to knowing why, only to have the answer snatched away by fate's dark sense of humor. In the days after, the tennis ball enigma took on legendary status. The family group chat buzzed with theories and memes – one showed a conspiracy theorist connecting red strings on a board, captioned: "Me trying to decipher Grandpa's tennis ball clue."

To this day, no one has a definitive answer why he needed those balls. But what began as a puzzling inside joke became a beloved family legend. Now, whenever someone encounters an unsolved little mystery – the missing TV remote, a cryptic comment from Dad – they shrug and say, "Chalk it up to the seventeen orange tennis balls." It's become shorthand for "one of life's unsolvable riddles." Frustrating, yes, but also oddly bonding. In a way, the old man pulled off one last grand prank: he ensured his family would chatter and collaborate long after he was gone, trying to decode his final riddle. Maybe that was the whole point – a final laugh that keeps going.

10.4 The Great-Grandmother's One-Word Finale

Not every mic-drop confession comes in the form of a long-held secret; sometimes it's simply a final mic-drop of an opinion. In one Midwestern American family, the great-grandmother had been the quiet matriarch for years. By quiet, we mean in her final months she rarely spoke at all, mostly sitting silently while family buzzed around her. She was in her 90s and pretty much checked out of the daily chatter – or so they thought. But mention college football and apparently some inner fire still burned. You see, for generations the whole family attended the same big state university, especially known for its football team. They practically bled the school colors. Until, that is, one renegade great-granddaughter – a teenager with an independent streak – decided to attend the arch-rival university across state lines. *Gasp!* The family, being generally supportive, only joked about her as the "traitor" or "rebel" in their proud lineage, never seriously – it was all good-natured ribbing.

Great-Grandma, an alumna of the old school back in the 1940s, hadn't voiced an opinion on the matter… given that she barely spoke at all.

One afternoon, the family gathered around Great-Grandma's hospice bed. The usual topics floated around – weather, memories, and of course some gentle teasing of the college turncoat in their midst. Someone joked, "Better not bring any rival-team pennants in here or Great-Gran might wake up just to scold you." Laughter followed and the teen rolled her eyes. Then, suddenly, Great-Grandma lifted her head, pointed at her great-granddaughter and in a raspy voice declared: "Traitor." With that, this ninety-something super-fan delivered her final verdict and promptly… well… died. She lay back and was gone, leaving everyone in stunned silence and then a chorus of *Did that really just happen?* around the room.

Once the initial shock passed, the family burst into laughter. It was just too perfectly absurd: she hadn't spoken in ages, yet this college decision was important enough to summon one final jab. It's as if Great-Grandma decided, "I may be at death's door, but I'm not leaving without repping my team." The timing and one-word mic drop were so on-point that even the great-granddaughter (newly anointed as the family rebel) had to smile through her tears. The family agreed Great-Gran went out in style.

News of this one-word send-off spread quickly through the family. By that evening, everyone had heard and the group chats were erupting with laughing emojis and mascot GIFs. The story instantly became family lore – recounted whenever the clan got together (often between football talk and dessert) – and everyone would burst out laughing. Even the great-granddaughter took it in stride – she embraced her new role as the family rebel, knowing she had a certain ghost now rooting for the other team.

If there's a lesson in this outrageous final word, it's that people can surprise you even at the very end. The quiet ones might just have the most epic finales. And it shows how deep even the silliest loyalties can run. Great-Grandma turned a somber moment into a comedic legacy. At a time of mourning, she left them with a story that perfectly captured her feisty spirit and the family's playful dynamic. It's a reminder that humor can be a powerful parting gift – even if it's as brief as a single shouted word.

10.5 The Half-Finished Treasure Hunt

Our final tale involves a grandfather who had a penchant for prankish drama – and a family now forever stuck in an unwinnable treasure hunt. In his final moments, one grandfather decided to drop a doozy of a cliffhanger. With his family gathered around, he beckoned his son closer and whispered, "I hid a wealth in the…" – then promptly expired mid-sentence. Just like that. He even wore a sly little smile as he went, as if he knew exactly what chaos he'd sown. The room was left in slack-jawed disbelief.

After the initial shock, the family sprang into action – half mourning, half sleuthing. That very day, a few grandkids grabbed shovels and started digging "just in case." An aunt tapped on walls listening for secret compartments, and an uncle waved a metal-detector app on his phone around the house (for the record, those don't really work). It was chaotic, yes – but also a strangely comic diversion amid the grief.

Eventually, they had to laugh. Of course Grandpa might have done this on purpose – it was exactly his style. The mental image of him chuckling from the afterlife while they tore the house apart was as infuriating as it was hilarious. Maybe *nothing* was hidden at all; perhaps his true parting gift was a bit of mystery and mischief to bring the family together one last time.

Family group chats later immortalized the saga with plenty of tongue-in-cheek treasure hunt jokes. Eventually they gave up the search, agreeing that Grandpa had gotten the last laugh. To this day, "I hid a wealth in the…" has become a family catchphrase. If someone leaves a story unfinished or teases a surprise, the others immediately shout, "…in the *what*, Grandpa?!" – always good for a chuckle.

In the end, through this final prank, Grandpa managed to do what he'd always done – bring his family together (albeit in exasperation) to share a memorable adventure. In a poetic way, he *did* leave them a wealth: not money, but a story they'll be telling for years. Sometimes the real treasure is the laughter we find along the way.

10.6 Bringing It All Together

These five tales prove that truth is often stranger – and funnier – than fiction. What could have been solemn final moments instead became comedies of errors and revelation: a grandmother's lifetime of owl gifts born from one misunderstanding; a grandfather whose famous recipe was actually store-bought all along; a dying man whose "17 orange tennis balls" secret died with him; a great-grandma who mustered a one-word zinger ("Traitor!") at the very end; and a grandfather who left his kin chasing an unfinished treasure clue.

Beyond the laughs, there's something heartwarming in these confessions. They show that even at the end of life, people still delight in surprise and connection – sometimes through mischief, sometimes through long-delayed honesty. These stories encourage us to embrace the absurdity: communicate more openly (stop an owl-gift trend before it snowballs), avoid putting loved ones on unrealistic pedestals (their "famous" meatballs might be store-bought), and don't take rivalries too seriously (if Great-Gran calls you a traitor with her last breath, just chalk it up as a loving tease).

In today's era of constant sharing, these tales stand out as refreshingly human and unscripted – the kind of anecdotes that get retold at every family reunion (and maybe even shared online for the world to laugh at). They remind us that our relatives are full of surprises right up to the end, and that humor and love often go hand in hand. So next time you're baffled by a loved one's quirky request or long-held secret, take a page from these stories. Smile, laugh if you can, and maybe ask a follow-up question or two *before* it's too late. Life is short and family is crazy, so enjoy the ride, oddball confessions and all. And perhaps double-check that Grandma actually likes owls before buying her that owl-shaped tea cozy.

Epilogue

We have reached the final page of this carnival of confessions, and what a ride it has been. Each turn of the page brought another jaw-dropping family secret, an outrageous scandal, or a deathbed revelation that left us laughing and gasping. Now, as the dust settles, we find something tender at the heart of it all: a reminder that every family has its quirks and hidden chapters, and that sharing them can set us free.

We giggled at eccentric uncles leading double lives and teared up when grandmothers revealed long-lost loves on their deathbeds. Beneath the absurdity and drama was an emotional core anyone can recognize. The outrageous stories weren't just played for laughs; they resonated because they carried the weight of real feelings—love, regret, hope, and a desire for understanding. By baring these secrets, the storytellers found catharsis and a dash of forgiveness. And as readers, we discovered a comforting truth: we're not alone in our family's crazy dance.

We honor the fearless spirit it takes to tell the truth. Not everyone ends up announcing a secret identity or a hidden fortune in chocolate coins on their deathbed, but the impulse behind those revelations feels familiar. It's that deep human need to be seen and accepted without the burden of our disguises. We all hold onto secrets—some silly, some heavy—waiting for the right time (or the last possible moment) to spill out. The characters in these pages let it all out in dramatic, hilarious ways.

Through their courage and impeccable comic timing, they remind us that honesty, even when delivered with laughter, can heal old wounds.

So as we close this book of wild family secrets, let's raise a toast to truth in all its outrageous glory—and to the mothers and fathers, siblings and spouses who dared to unveil their hidden selves and found liberation in it, showing us that vulnerability can be uproariously funny and deeply moving. May these tales inspire us to embrace our eccentric histories and share our stories when the time is right. In that act of sharing, we build a bridge across generations, uniting us in a shared humanity that laughs, cries, and ultimately heals together. In the end, truth really is stranger than fiction—and it's the one thing that can set us all free. It leaves us with hearts lighter, spirits brighter, and a family of readers who've seen it all— and still smile at what it means to be human.

www.ingramcontent.com/pod-product-compliance
Lightning Source LLC
Chambersburg PA
CBHW061753120626
46550CB00005B/1981